ADAPTIVE LEADERSHIP IN ORGANIZATIONAL UNCERTAINTY & DYNAMICS

A PRACTICAL LEADERSHIP GUIDE THAT HELPS INDIVIDUALS ADAPT TO CHANGING BUSINESS ENVIRONMENTS.

DR. AMIT DAS

To

All my bosses who made a difference in my professional career.

This life is a wonderful gift .. accept it, embrace it.
It starts with a new day .. wake up and greet it.
Life is a challenge .. take it head on and meet it.
Full of opportunity .. use it, don't waste it.

This life is a mystery .. unfold it, solve it.
It starts with meaning .. wake up and understand it.
Life is a goal .. take it head on and achieve it.
Full of promise .. fulfill it but keep it.

Life is a struggle .. take it head on and fight it.
Full of sorrow .. sorry, just overcome it.
This life is precious .. hold it, treasure it,
It starts with hope .. wake up and feel it.

Life is a choice .. take it head on and make it.
Full of knowledge .. use it, don't abuse it.
This life is adventurous .. enjoy it, explore it.
It starts with a duty .. wake up and perform it.

-Anonymous

Contents

Foreword

Leadership Must Be Adaptable In The Face Of Volatile, Uncertain, Complex, And Ambiguous Change.

"Change is good. It's also often hard. But to succeed in business, you must run toward it."-Anonymous

Dear Readers,

Thank you for taking the time to learn more about the adaptive leadership in organizational uncertainties and dynamism. The author recognizes that intelligent, motivated individuals like you have special gifts to give the world, but it's difficult to do in this VUCA business environment. The author has spent his entire professional career assisting managers in increasing their productivity, which he describes as the capacity to make progress on the results that matter most to them professionally and individually. This book *"ALOUD"* aims to teach you how critical it is to be adaptive every day toward achieving the things that matter most to you, leaving no stone unturned, and to develop a mindset of seeing the most overlooked aspects of life not only for what they are or appear to be, but also for what they could be. Through his profession, he's seen that the vast majority of time management advice offered doesn't help you enhance your life. Adaptive leadership has been defined as a critical leadership method for dealing with adaptive, rather than technical or predictable, difficulties, which are particularly common in complex situations. The book *"ALOUD"* supports a new social contract, a rejuvenation of your civic life at a time when you most need it.

Change may be frightening, disturbing, and disconcerting. Fear, tension, resentment, and resistance can arise even when change is anticipated or desired. These reactions to change are frequently perceived by leaders as a hurdle that must be overcome. Adaptive leaders must be able to determine when to enter the conflict and when to exit and observe from the sidelines. The author of *"ALOUD"* explores many notions of flexible and adaptive leadership, as well as why such leadership is necessary in today's enterprises. Then numerous study streams that give helpful knowledge regarding flexible and adaptable leadership are briefly presented. Although a complete and exhaustive examination was not possible, the author summarizes his main findings and offers some practical advice for leaders on how to become more flexible and adaptive in this VUCA corporate environment.

The only thing that stays the same in today's corporate climate is change, and change is more plentiful, quick, and complex than ever before. Change and upheaval are the new normal in today's corporate world. Companies, and even entire sectors, can be turned completely upside down in an instant. Adaptability is no longer just a desirable trait in a leader; it's a necessity. Adaptable leaders understand that leading and managing change is a need in today's business world, and they are constantly looking for new methods to solve new problems, learn new skills, and take on new challenges with a sense of grounded inventiveness.

This book outlines the importance of adaptive leadership, clearing your head of clutter, and sticking to a single-point agenda. The days of traditional, stability-oriented organizations are numbered. Organizations built for both stability and dynamism with networks of teams and people-centered cultures governed by common goals and co-created value for all stakeholders are replacing them. The Business Dictionary defines " *Adaptive Leadership"* as a *"Chameleon-like personality"* capable of keeping up with fast changes in its environment.

During the times of upheaval and uncertainty, many companies recognize the need for speed. Leaders perceive an opportunity to accelerate their firms' pace by doing even more in the areas mentioned above in the future. Respondents most typically cite more efficient decision making, clearer communication, and the use of technology to better engage consumers and staff when asked about the key chances to attain higher speed. The author offers the most effective tactics and step-by-step instructions for you to construct your own particular road to excellence in this book. You'll also find better methods to collaborate with colleagues, respond more effectively to coaching and mentoring, and become more positive and self-directed in your thoughts and actions, resulting in more personal and professional pleasure. This book attempts to provide insights into the many pathways, courses, and drives that world-class enterprises have constructed in order to achieve the pinnacles of greatness. This book provides cutting-edge material, including innovative and unusual study aids as well as fresh, thought-provoking content, with an emphasis on integrating corporate agility, or adaptiveness, into practical management.

Regardless of the audience, reading this book puts the reader on a unique and advantageous platform to connect in a more intelligent and successful manner. This book is well-researched and educational for people of all ages and genders. This book *"ALOUD"*, is a quest to perceive even the most mundane things in a new light. Its goal is to assist you to harness your capacity to become more adaptive and use it to your advantage in order to rise above the mediocre tides in all aspects of your life. It reveals numerous methods for intentionally cultivating a mindset that refuses to be superficial about life.

To survive and prosper, a leader must be able to foresee, plan for, respond to, and adapt to problems and opportunities. It goes beyond risk management to take a more comprehensive view of an individual's health and performance. An *"adaptive leadership"* is one that not only survives, but also flourishes in the long run, surviving the test of time. Techniques work well for the simple and the complicated, but not so well for the complex. The complex requires a new strategy, with the goal of making the organization being led more nimble and self-organizing. Dr. Amit Das has designed a straightforward and step-by-step method for Leadership based on his previous work, complex adaptive leadership, while challenging and questioning the reader to be more successful and less busy. This book *"ALOUD"* will appeal to practitioners who want to increase their leadership effectiveness. It is an essential tool for the time-pressed leader and manager. It will also be of interest to leadership students and academics.

Every company relies on its leadership to strengthen, organize, and shift resources in order to make the most efficient and effective use of them in order to enhance returns on investment and develop adaptiveness. Dr. Amit Das provides a step-by-step approach in this book on how to create an excellent adaptive culture at your firm. The author demonstrates how to uncover your hidden culture, transform ideals into actions, and open up communication across layers. To keep your culture thriving for the long term, the author emphasizes the significance of being clear from the top, building trust, and providing support structures. As Dr. Amit Das demonstrates in his book, by building your culture, you can increase communication, raise morale, encourage trust, and keep negativity at bay within your team.

The author provides businesses with a step-by-step strategy for analyzing, creating, and implementing iterative adaptive cultural transformation, with each success building on prior achievements. As a result, the company continues to adapt in ways that reduce stress, encourage learning, and promote organizational wellness. Indeed, it may have increased as businesses realize their present systems are incapable of keeping up with the current rate of change. Transformation is not without danger, but adopting agility may mitigate this by giving organizations the resilience they need to deal with constant change. Consider whether your processes are flexible enough. Could your essential business systems adapt quickly to significant operational changes?

There is no exact formula for predicting the future of any industry; nonetheless, business executives can envision the next day based on the unique qualities of each organization. The book "ALOUD" draws on first-hand experience from high-performance operations to deliver vital adaptive leadership lessons as well as clear, accessible, and practical insights on managing teams in any corporate setting. This book provides a new and fascinating viewpoint on the factors that influence team and organizational greatness. Dr. Amit Das, the book's author, has a unique combination of expertise and insight, having worked as a management consultant. His insights and interviews from business sectors are used to demonstrate the obstacles to high performance and leadership.

The materials include a performance model that can be applied to a wide range of organizations, focusing on people's attitudes rather than skills; a process for closing the gap between desired and actual outcomes; how to accelerate performance in real time; exhibiting a set of behaviours that the capacity of an organization to function efficiently, adapt properly, adjust correctly, and grow from within is referred to as organizational health. The author also looks at whether great leaders are born or made, how lean ideas are used differently in various organizations, and why clever individuals fail so often after being promoted to management positions. Take a path that leads to significant performance increases and a great culture where everyone is prepared to succeed with this leadership. Just like strategy, writing a book takes deep contemplation to narrate a theory in a very lucid manner. Hence, the author could establish his thought process for readers.

So, happy reading and learning to all readers.

Carpe diem.

Dr. Amit Das

Preface

Leadership Becomes More Difficult When Competing Values Exist.

"You can't build an adaptable organization without adaptable people--and individuals change only when they have to, or when they want to." -Gary Hamel

Change is unavoidable in today's enterprises. It means in business, change is the only constant, although it is rarely as unexpected or as overpowering as it has been in 2022. During their careers, the majority of these executives claim to have been through many acquisitions, mergers, reorganizations, or other significant organizational changes. They show that the rate and magnitude of change are both increasing. Recognizing that change is unavoidable is not the same as effectively dealing with it. Many leaders have little or no awareness of or training in navigating the change process, despite the fact that their capacity to react to, manage, control, and promote change is critical to their success.

Situations that are volatile, uncertain, complex, and uncertain have never been harsher, and the need for adaptable leadership has never been more critical. But how can adaptive leadership work in the real world?What is the best way to teach it through leadership development programs? Which tools help it improve its practice and teaching? What are the connections between adaptive leadership and other important ideas and practices? This book *"ALOUD"* answers these and other issues by demonstrating how adaptable leadership methods are used to handle some of the world's most serious challenges—political and cultural divides, remote work, and crisis management—across a wide range of industries.

Traditional leadership patterns were beginning to fail even before the unprecedented difficulties of 2020. You saw an obvious need for it as companies advanced and expanded against a backdrop of continual social, technical, and cultural development, and you saw the need to move away from management methods that place a deterministic focus on a single leader. The coronavirus pandemic has upended a number of industries, from hospitality to energy, that appeared positioned for success in the new decade until lately. Businesses are now scrambling to pick up the debris while navigating an uncertain future. Under normal conditions, change management is a difficult task. Accepting change is the definition of adaptability. Adaptability is the practice of fine-tuning methods. While agility or adaptability has always been crucial in the modern workplace, it is now more important than ever.

Global pandemics, business restructurings, downsizings, increased globalization, and market upheavals are just a few of the unexpected challenges that leaders and their organizations must negotiate. Another driver of transition is the rapid evolution of technology, which necessitates continual retraining for individuals and organizations due to rising rates of obsolescence and replacement. Additionally, the people that make up organizations, work groups, and teams change regularly. Gradual changes in the external environment can result in a new danger or opportunity for the company. New rivals, new technology, social and cultural changes, new legal or regulatory rules, changes in economic situations, and changes in consumer wants and preferences are just a few examples. Instead of just improving a current strategy or relying on a planned contingency plan, successful adaptation to such changes sometimes necessitates an imaginative new approach.

In today's complicated VUCA settings, striking a balance between chaos and rigorous structure is critical. It might be difficult to create and maintain the ideal environment. Culture, ownership, mentality, feedback, and long-term objectives are all important. The leader must be able to handle a variety of situations, particularly new, changing, and ambiguous ones. It is connected with mode four leaders who have the agility to function in any mode and, most crucially, perceive things from many perspectives. The capacity to think in a variety of ways is what gives such leaders their flexibility. If you know that changes are occurring in the competitive environment, you can quickly determine who will be most resistant to the adjustment in priorities required to manage the new scenario. This book *"ALOUD"* is for management teams that want to improve their organization's ability to adapt to and respond to environmental changes. The majority of leadership assumptions are founded on a deterministic worldview. If you do X, you should receive Y; this procedure can be applied to almost anything, and more complex situations may be analyzed for improved decision-making.

Chameleons are wonderful animals. They have been around for almost 100 million years. Chameleons change color to blend in with their environment or to stand out from predators and other chameleons. Their eyes can stare in opposing directions at the same time, which helps them see predators and food. They can predict and adapt to a wide range of settings, including hostile and rapidly changing ecosystems like rainforests and deserts. Unlike other animals, such as dodos or dinosaurs, which became extinct when their habitat changed dramatically, they have demonstrated the capacity to not only adapt and survive, but also thrive. To put it another way, these species are actually adaptable. Being adaptive does not imply that you are unaware of your identity. Chameleons only change color when they need to. If they're on a leaf, they're green if they should be, and if they're on a branch, they're brown if they should be. It understands what hue to show when it isn't near anything it needs to adjust to. The chameleon was aware of his own nature and content with who he was. It is quite similar for a leader to be adaptable as well. Leaders, like chameleons, are aware of who they are, their values, and their skills. However, it understands the need to adjust to changes in their surroundings. Leadership has evolved in the era of knowledge and information, and it has become more interested in finding ways to survive that allow them to keep up with the environment and the next digital age, which will put it on the cusp of leadership wisdom.

To be effective, a leader must strike a balance between goals that require difficult compromises, such as reliability and efficiency, and the requirement for creative adaptability to new threats and possibilities. Competing ideals and tradeoffs can sometimes result in actions that are diametrically opposed (e.g., controlling vs. empowering). Another example of flexible leadership is a leader's ability to balance opposing ideals and contrary styles of conduct in a way that is acceptable for the occasion. Moving from one post to another in the same company or to a higher one in a different organization is common in a management career. Different sorts of management jobs, as well as positions in another company with a diverse objective or culture, require different patterns of conduct for effective leadership. By recognizing these crucial shifts, describing the inner tensions they cause, and giving advice for effective navigation, the author gives a framework for dealing with and responding to them. This outside-in approach identifies the most important leadership issues that CEOs will encounter when they mobilize their businesses to successfully adapt to competitive and environmental change. According to this book, strategy is leadership because environmental changes necessitate alterations in strategic goals, which result in a constant pattern of resistance.

One of the pillars of adaptation is the ability to remain hopeful while remaining realistic. Successful adapters see change as an opportunity rather than a danger. They believe they can maintain their effectiveness in the new context. Managers' confidence in their ability to be effective during times of transition appears to be boosted by optimism. It's arguable whether optimism can be taught, but the next time you're in a circumstance that requires change, try discovering something positive and building on it. Make a note of the opportunities given by the transition and share them with the rest of the organization.

Adaptive leadership, if it existed at all, was not a well-known notion during Abraham Lincoln's time. Nonetheless, Lincoln had certain adaptable leadership qualities that are worth considering. His openness to tolerating variety was one of these traits. Lincoln is alleged to have appointed his enemies to the cabinet on purpose. He desired to engage their divergent viewpoints in order to guide the country to the greatest answers. He was always open to criticism and discussion as a leader. In addition, Lincoln was empathic and fast at forming ties with the people he led. He effectively had an open-door policy, allowing individuals to come to him and talk about their problems. His compassionate posture and attentive ears helped him acquire the respect of people around him.

Management and leadership are two separate entities. Management is concerned with dealing with complexity, people, and tasks, whereas leadership is concerned with dealing with change and ensuring that the team works together to achieve common goals. The most effective leaders are able to adapt quickly to changing situations and utilize the appropriate strategy for each occasion. Poor leaders, on the other hand, fail to change appropriately in dynamic situations, resulting in chaos and confusion. What happens if you put pressure on a crystal glass? It usually becomes weaker over time and finally breaks. Crystal glasses, like many other items and living things, are delicate. What is the polar opposite of delicate? Strong, tenacious, and adaptable come to mind. Being robust, resilient, and flexible, on the other hand, is not the polar opposite of being fragile.

Leaders that learn and adapt to problems in a volatile, unpredictable, complex, and ambiguous (VUCA) business environment have a significant competitive edge. Leaders must adjust as well, frequently making significant changes because their roles might be procedural and rule-driven. The author of "ALOUD" explains how to apply systems thinking to any framework in order to become more adaptable and effective in a rapidly changing world. Anyone who runs an organization or an organizational endeavor will tell you that things are changing quickly and that the difficulties you all face are becoming more complicated. Leaders must be adaptable and sensitive to the fast-changing world in order to flourish in this VUCA environment. This begins with paying attention to critical input that will lead you to the result you aim to achieve via your organizational efforts. It is your responsibility as a systems leader to build an organization that can adapt to the difficulties it confronts on a daily basis.

In this book *"ALOUD"*, the author will discuss how you may become a leader who thoroughly knows how you think, allowing your team to tackle any problem, issue, or scenario and turn insight into unique ideas for real effect and change. Systems thinking entails attempting to comprehend the systems that surround you. To do more than just respond to circumstances as they occur. Instead, consider how the world truly works. In today's fast-changing competitive VUCA world, merely pursuing efficiency would not be enough. So the author will show you a framework for establishing adaptable companies that are quick and agile in responding to market changes.

Leaders must also realize that organizational results are not something that can be generated directly, but rather indirectly, through instilling a set of simple norms that govern each group member's work. To develop system-level behavior, you must concentrate on the underlying rules that generate it. The issue is that CEOs, administrators, and other organizational leaders are always striving to get more out of their teams and organizations in order to improve both internal efficiency and outward influence. They want to work smarter and leave a bigger impression on the world faster. The issue is that humans do not act like a collection of gears. Their intentions are often mixed, and you're all aware that they may participate in more subtle types of resistance, which gears do not.

The majority of organizational challenges you confront are caused by gaps between how organizations actually operate and how you believe they work. As a result of feedback, these things get more aligned. It is the leader's responsibility to foster a culture that values and changes in response to input. Failure must be considered a chance to learn. To compete, people must be encouraged to try and retest their ideas, as well as given room to iterate. This is adaptation, and adaptable organizations are the result of adaptive leadership.

Are you a leader who can adapt?

Because the world is changing at a breakneck pace, leaders come in a variety of sizes and forms. If you've been keeping up with the newest leadership trends, you've definitely already heard about several techniques and ideals that have proven successful for many current and prospective business leaders. To be honest, there is no right or wrong way to lead, as long as you have the best interests of your team and your company at heart. But what if your squad isn't going to stay the same for long? It will shift. And it's not only your team that will alter; it's your workplace culture, your market, everything. This is when you put one of your essential leadership characteristics, namely adaptability, to the test. In this piece, author'll offer some statistics on why and how adaptability is a critical component of leadership, regardless of the team or organization with which you're working. In addition, you'll discover some of my finest ideas and methods for being an adaptive leader in a fast-paced sector. Most significantly, flexibility is changing to suit new conditions and obstacles, which will ensure your company's or organization's success. Why is it vital for a leader to be adaptable? Change is unavoidable. Everything grows and evolves into something better, including the workplace dynamic, corporate strategy, and technological advancements.

Adapting and responding is the only way to survive as a leader and face the complexity of change, whether you like it or not.

The author emphasized the need for continuous professional growth. To avoid extinction, his formula asserts that an organization's rate of learning must be equal to or greater than the rate of change in the environment. Fortunately, learning possibilities abound in today's environment, and this richness should be embraced as well as utilized. Adaptive leaders encourage learning by cultivating a culture that appreciates it and actively shares it.

Acknowledgements

At the outset I will thank to my family for supporting me throughout the journey of writing my book and encouraging me to live my dreams- my son has always been instrumental in giving his inspiration to complete the writing of this book. Despite the fact that I am listed as the author of this book, "The Secret Of Adaptable Organization" would not have been published if I had depended entirely on my own talents. To create this book required more than a village—it took a family of dedicated and caring people who were always prepared to lend a hand.

Writing a book while working full-time is no simple task, so I'd want to express my gratitude to my amazing coworkers, who act as mentors and cheerleaders in equal measure. Thank you, too, to the rest of the accumentor team for your patience and unflinching support while I worked on this book!

Thank you to everyone who has listened to me argue for doing everything you can to make your life, including your work life, more progressive. I appreciate everyone's assistance throughout the process. This book would not have been possible without each of you having had an impact on my life in some manner.

Lastly, I would like to thank all the people whom I have been associated, you gave me power. I would like to thank Notion Press for publishing my book. At last thank you all for gifting your time to read out this book.

I'd want to convey my heartfelt appreciation to the Almighty God for bestowing his blessings and being so gracious.

CHAPTER ONE

FUNDAMENTALS

Thrive in Understanding Different Points Of View And Ideas

"Adaptability is not imitation. It means the power of resistance and assimilation."- Mahatma Gandhi

Adaptability is essential to generating progress and helps the organization and its members stay effective and productive through times of change and uncertainty. Leaders must not only be flexible themselves, but they must also be able to detect adaptation in their personnel. This ability aids leaders in selecting individuals who are best suited to change-related work and who can motivate and serve as role models for others during the transition period that comes with any new project. Adaptability is therefore critical to the effectiveness and success of leaders. This is most likely not breaking news to you. Despite the fact that the need for adaptability in leaders is now widely accepted, little is understood about what adaptability actually entails. Little research has been done on the specific behaviors that define adaptability up to now.

If leaders can obtain a better understanding of these behaviors, they will be able to not only recognize them but also take the first steps toward creating flexibility in themselves and others. Many executives fail due to their inability or unwillingness to change. This could be due to their incapacity or unwillingness to adapt their management style, as well as their personal fear of change.

Given the chaotic and uncertain global climate that organizations confront on both a macro and local level, planning for the future has never been more challenging. When the dust settles from the COVID-19 problem, you might be confronted with a new environment that may differ radically from what you are used to in terms of consumer behavior, business models, and the responsibilities of the public and private sectors. The longer and more severe the crisis, the more likely it is that dramatic changes will characterize the new world of tomorrow. The author has highlighted the variety of probable situations businesses may encounter, as well as guidelines and best practices for making strategic decisions in tomorrow's new environment, based on insights from client interactions and internal specialists.

Flexible and adaptive leadership is critical when unexpected occurrences disrupt work or cause an urgent problem that demands the leader's attention. According to a descriptive study on management activities and decision-making, most managers spend a significant amount of time dealing with difficulties and disturbances that potentially disrupt work. A crisis is an uncommon and urgent situation with potentially significant consequences, such as serious accidents, explosions, natural catastrophes, equipment malfunctions, product flaws, supply shortages, health problems, employee strikes, sabotage, or a terrorist attack.

After a time of rapid adaptation, businesses throughout the world are considering what the new world may look like in the next few years. Both very probable trends (such as increased working from home and more e-commerce) and other high-impact trends whose future growth is considerably more unpredictable will change the world of tomorrow. Grouping these tendencies into two dimensions is a useful way to think about them: trends in economic structural and policy transformations, typified by nations and major corporations seeking to mitigate global interdependency concerns. trends in residents' long-term behavioral adjustments as consumers and employees, deriving from their early experiences of social isolation and lockdown.

In 2022, global businesses plan to become more adaptable in response to rising digital experience expectations. While 90% of CEOs believe their company must be able to adapt quickly and at scale in order to provide value to their customers, consumers continue to perceive brands as falling short. According to the report, 91% of corporate leaders have made efforts to enhance customer experiences in the last year, with 84% undertaking more experimentation than ever during the epidemic, testing and iterating to discover what worked and what didn't. While 9 out of 10 respondents believe their company must be able to adapt quickly and on a large scale in order to provide value to customers, only half (46%) believe they are already adaptable. Furthermore, 78% of consumers believe businesses could do a better job of changing to match current demands. 70% of corporate executives agree that they cannot optimize as soon as they would want, and roughly the same number 72% express difficulty scaling efforts to suit global demands, highlighting the disparity between brands' objectives and purpose in relation to the adapatable digital experience they presently offer.

As you face the expanding demands of their positions, the leaders you deal with frequently describe feeling trapped, ill-equipped, or overwhelmed. It's understandable to feel this way when our world's complexity exceeds our *"complexity of thought,"* as Robert Kegan and Lisa Lahey describe in their book Immunity to Change. To put it another way, since the mid-1950s, computing capacity has expanded more than a trillion-fold, while our brains have remained constant. Leaders must first learn to lead themselves in order to effectively lead others in more complicated situations. Despite the fact that each leader has their own set of circumstances, we've identified six tactics that can help you grow, adapt, and overcome more complicated issues.

Adaptability necessitates effective change interpretation, and the first step is admitting that change has occurred. The important parts of the transition that successful adapters address are how a new vision will produce new markets, competitors, and organizational positions. It's also crucial to figure out how the change will affect the organization's operations. Another facet of cognitive flexibility is the ability to generate alternative strategies. Adaptable leaders may let go of old roles and concepts, recognize and embrace new roles, and devise new tactics and action plans to meet the consequences of the transition and the current situation. Divergent thinking is another aspect of cognitive flexibility, such as considering a completely new approach that turns a change into an advantage, or recognizing and putting to use the skills of new team members. Finally, cognitive adapters excel at transcending organizational boundaries; they analyze how the change will affect others and disseminate this knowledge to various organizational units and senior management.

Leaders that are skilled in the dispositional characteristics of adaptability inspire others in the organization or team to embrace change. As a method of acknowledging that change has occurred and new group dynamics will emerge, they encourage contributions from others, honestly congratulate others for their innovative ideas, and make formal introductions of individuals who are new to the organization or team.Personality-related adaptability also entails staying highly engaged during times of change – not *"checking out"* emotionally or physically, remaining enthusiastic and energetic, consistently and usefully contributing to new strategy brainstorming, and successfully integrating into a new team or working across new organizational boundaries. Effective leaders, on the other hand, enable the transition process to take place rather than rejecting emotions and negative reactions or being tough and rushing through change. Denial; resistance; investigation, questioning, and reaction; and, finally, commitment are common stages in change reactions. People can gain more adaptability in the face of change through this technique.

It's fine for managers to express their opposition to change—in fact, it's preferred—because suppressed emotions will ultimately arise and must be addressed. Resistance to change is natural, yet the emotional element of adaptation requires recognition and knowledge of change. When you admit your reluctance to a change, others in the organization can help you cope with it. At the same time, it's critical to keep emotions in check, retain a sense of balance, and stay on track. The emotional component of adaptation is addressing the feelings of others. Managers should encourage employees to communicate their sentiments about a change, whether they are favorable or negative, and should not be critical of such communication. One approach to achieving this is to schedule a weekly organizational or group meeting and allow everyone to express their ideas and feelings regarding the change that is taking place and the impact it is having.

Although the necessity for leaders to be adaptable is well recognised, little is known about what adaptation actually entails. If the capacity to lead and manage change is the key differentiator in today's increasingly fast-paced corporate environment, CEOs who can adapt to change rather than merely cope with it will consistently achieve exceptional results. Metathesiophobia, that's the tongue-twisting term for the dread of change, which most people will acknowledge having experienced if they're honest with themselves. Even when the change is minimal and the individual desires it, it can be unpleasant and disturbing—and hence terrifying. Fear is often accompanied by stress and resistance. Fearing and rejecting change, as well as refusing to venture into the unknown, may be fatal to leaders, their followers, and their organizations. The only thing that stays the same in today's corporate climate is change, and change is more unpredictable and complex than ever before.

As the global economy returns to normal, it's an exciting moment to be a white-shoe advisor, working with struggling businesses that need all the support they can get with growth, expenses, strategy, and execution. If there was ever any doubt about the importance of a leader's capacity to negotiate change, uncertainty, and disruption, the worldwide pandemic of 2020 proved it beyond a shadow of a doubt. While you all wish to avoid future pandemics, one thing is certain: you will not be able to escape increased complexity. Rather than avoiding these sentiments, you must learn to accept and embrace them as an inevitable component of the learning process. According to Microsoft CEO Satya Nadella, executives must move from a *"know it all"* to a *"learn it all"* approach. This adjustment in perspective might assist in alleviating the discomfort by relieving the strain on you to know everything.

The ability of managers to deal with this type of transition—losing familiar team members and dealing with new and unknown colleagues—has a significant impact on organizational efficiency and production. Change – and how they and their colleagues react to it – has become critical to their effectiveness and the success of their businesses, as leaders are well aware. In a poll conducted by Ernst & Young and Cap Gemini Ernst & Young, 86 CEOs identified the top three dangers that they and their businesses would face in the future years. Executives (19%) mentioned regulatory changes (38%), competitive dynamics (29%), and market uncertainty. All of these issues are linked to the transition.

New initiatives can be derailed or stifled before they get a chance, or just die on the vine, if leaders don't consider their own flexibility and that of their subordinates. When an organization's top leadership announces a new vision, for example, managers and their teams are expected to embrace it and propel it toward implementation as rapidly as feasible. to comprehend and embrace the new vision, as well as to motivate subordinates to follow suit.

As the speed of change in businesses accelerates, most managers and administrators will need to be more flexible and adaptable in their leadership. Increased globalization and international commerce; rapid technological change; changing cultural values; a more diverse workforce; more outsourcing; new forms of social networking; increased use of virtual interaction; more visibility of leadership actions; and concern for outcomes other than profits are examples of changes that increase the need for flexibility, adaptation, and innovation by leaders. Although there is currently a lack of studies specifically focused on flexible and adaptable leadership, interest in the topic is growing as its value becomes more apparent. Furthermore, because subordinates differ in terms of experience, talents, beliefs, and requirements, a leader's conduct with various individuals should vary. For subordinates with good talents and a strong dedication to work objectives, for example, increased delegation is suitable. When a subordinate's talents and motivations vary over time, flexibility is also essential. Using the same scenario, greater delegation will be acceptable as a subordinate acquires experience and confidence.

Different sorts of management jobs, as well as positions in another company with a diverse objective or culture, require different patterns of conduct for effective leadership. Making these job transfers successfully is another sign of flexible and adaptable leadership. Finding inventive methods to cope with new issues and possibilities is frequently part of being flexible and adaptable, yet the sorts of decisions and actions required for effective leadership may not be compatible with standard organizational position expectations. Role expectations can sometimes be founded on outdated ideas or inappropriate norms and values (e.g., gender role stereotypes, centralized authority, intolerance for any failures, or promotion based on seniority rather than performance). It may be necessary for a leader to persuade individuals to shift their assumptions and views about what is proper and successful in order to extend their options, especially when the benefits of creative techniques are not immediately apparent.

Using everyone's abilities rather than simply those of top-level leaders is what an ideal talent mix includes. A clear charter ensures that the organization or team adheres to well-defined goals, responsibilities, and ground rules, while trust fosters strong links between workers, employers, and clients. There are various paradigms and definitions of leadership agility. The paradigm of one distinctive leadership style is slipping away in current times, and each scenario will require a different sort of leader. The team's agility is becoming increasingly important. As a result, leadership agility is built on an adaptive team that can pivot in a new direction as the situation requires. Nowadays, teams are formed swiftly and then disbanded just as quickly. They must promptly establish contact with the project leader, be given full authority to make choices, and complete the assignment. If agility is not fostered, inflexible leaders can severely slow down growth. Here are three methods for forming adaptive teams:

"We cannot address the problems with the same mindset that created them," -Einstein observed.

You are to blame for your current circumstances. Here's something to think about for a bit. Your systems have been tuned to provide the results you're seeing now. If your work efforts are constantly over budget or late, you've established a system that not only produces these results, but it is optimized to produce them. You must modify the system in order to change the outcomes. The art of adaptive leadership is establishing the ideal environment for self-organization. An atmosphere in which adaptive teams cooperate, learn from one another, receive immediate feedback from users, and are committed to quality and continual improvement. He or she neither micromanages nor creates unlimited freedom for the individuals.

Leaders frequently state that they favor transparency. What they truly mean is that they want to know what their teams are up to all of the time. Leaders who are honest about their own work—sharing information about what they're working on, bigger corporate goals, and the priorities that should direct their teams' work—are required for adaptive leadership. Of course, teams must be capable in order to be effective in solving their own problems. Employees benefit from both formal and embedded learning opportunities, such as work shadowing and job rotation, provided by great adaptive leaders. Adaptive leaders don't wait for a slowdown to grow their people—they know those are rare—instead, they use busy moments to stretch and challenge team members to contribute in new ways and through new responsibilities that stretch and challenge them.

Learning is impossible without some risk and failure. While conventional leaders may seek for green lights on the dashboard progress report, adaptive leaders encourage individuals to be open about where they've pushed themselves and where they may be struggling—the truth. Customers must be involved in the process for adaptive work approaches to be successful. Great adaptive leaders make it easier for customers to participate. Consumers' expectations are defined, opportunities and workplaces where customers may be present are provided, and customers are given the time they require.

Working on one project at a time, for example, is an important aspect of adaptive. Leaders must sometimes push back on the business to ensure that adaptive teams are not overburdened and can thrive by prioritizing projects and outcomes. Performance is measured by adaptive leaders. Measurement, monitoring, and management are all intertwined. Great adaptive leaders encourage teams to measure their own results in addition to tracking their own measures. They track factors like meeting time, number of projects, customer happiness, team trust, and more, in addition to velocity, the gold standard of adaptive measurement. They know how the team is doing so they can provide feedback, eliminate roadblocks, and create possibilities for growth.

Feedback is an important aspect of adaptive development. Great adaptive leaders provide feedback while also empowering their teams to provide and accept input. They assist the team in maintaining contact with the organization in order to obtain critical feedback from internal customers and the firm as a whole. Adaptive leaders serve as mentors and coaches for the teams they manage. Because adaptive is a new method of working in most organizations, outstanding adaptive leaders must educate the rest of the organization on work procedures, eliminate barriers, and establish team boundaries. Working as a team, for example, is an important aspect of adaptive.

For teams, adaptive leadership necessitates new levels of empowerment, enablement, and development. Adaptive teams are learning new work practices at the same time as executives who are ensuring success in the new adaptive environment. You will not last long if you are unable to adapt to change. This is becoming increasingly critical as the pace of change accelerates. To allow faster and better adaptability to change, a leader must comprehend not only the people around them, but also themselves.

- ***So, what exactly is the adaptive problem?***
- ***What stands in the way of adaptation?***
- ***How can quick adaptation be made possible?***

When it comes to this, look to visionary and transformational leadership for inspiration. Leaders who put in time during a disruption achieve cost-effective results with long-term benefits. Adaptive leaders put their followers first. Adaptive leaders inspire their staff to recognize change and respond to it with easy solutions. They assist others in completing *"the work"* required to overcome the obstacles. Great leaders build strong, dependable, and flexible teams by utilizing this adaptive talent.

Power Points

- Leaders must not only be flexible themselves, but they must also be able to detect adaptation in their personnel.
- Leaders that are skilled in the dispositional characteristics of adaptability inspire others in the organization or team to embrace change.
- Fear is often accompanied by stress and resistance.

CHAPTER TWO

UNCERTAINTIES & DYNAMISM

No Organization Is Immune To Disruption.

"Learn to adjust yourself to the conditions you have to endure, but make a point of trying to alter or correct conditions so that they are most favorable to you."
-William Frederick Book

Many businesses have been pushed to their limits, and in some cases, to the brink of bankruptcy, in the previous year. Today, no sector or company is immune to disruption, but many are unprepared to adapt rapidly enough to keep up with the pace of change. Their systems have disintegrated due to intense strain on operations, supply chains, and demand, and any notion of collaboration among their ranks has been tossed to the wind. Working in crisis mode is, of course, neither sustainable nor desirable. Many company executives are now wondering how they can maintain momentum post-crisis and ensure their firms' future adaptability.

What makes today's corporate environment unique is how ubiquitous dynamism is. The rate of change is now affecting everyone, not just the so-called disrupted industries or particular aspects of your firm; it's occurring in every industry and at every level of business. Because technology is so ingrained in every aspect of our operations, it is at the center of much of the changing environment. Technology changes the way you communicate, market, drive your business processes, shape product development and manufacturing, and determines how you connect with your customers for many organizations. However, it isn't having the greatest technology that gives you a competitive edge; it's enterprises that adapt technology to fit their strategic goals.

Many interrelated aspects make up complex tasks, some of which are unknown and alter in unanticipated ways over time. Furthermore, an action or change in one dimension might have unintended and exaggerated consequences. While there are many points of view on these issues, no obvious answers exist. As a result, complex problem-solving solutions are usually discovered by trial and error and need the desire, humility, and capacity to act, learn, and adapt. Many high achievers have an action bias and grow dissatisfied fast when confronted with problems for which there is no obvious answer or clear line of action. Leaders must not give in to the need for a rapid answer.

The COVID-19 epidemic hastened the pace of change, highlighting the degree of globalization and the interconnectedness of technology, society, and the environment in new ways. This paradigm change has also exposed the frailty of individuals formerly regarded as industry leaders. However, not all businesses have faltered throughout the epidemic. Some businesses, such as so-called *"work from home"* businesses and e-commerce giants, were in the right place at the right time. Others have managed to stay afloat thanks to a strong emphasis on resilience, financial stability, and contingency preparation. Even fewer have strategically leveraged the crisis to develop or grow their businesses. These businesses have shown an exceptional capacity to adapt swiftly to changing conditions. Such businesses are ideally positioned to compete in the present, future, and beyond.

How can people transition from crisis mode to proactive thinking?

The epidemic has brought attention to the need for businesses to be adaptive, but business executives have long recognized this requirement. They had to deal with various problems even before the chaos of 2020. Most corporate executives believe they have been in a perpetual state of *"transformation"* for the past two decades, and many are weary of hearing the phrase. The secret is to maintain a constant state of flexibility. Every business leader understands that in order to thrive in the long run, their organization must adapt. The true challenge isn't effectively converting your firm on a one-time basis; it's writing the capacity to adapt and transform into the DNA of the company. It's about creating a mechanism or reaction to cope with any crisis that arises, whether it's a financial, technical, environmental, or health-related one.

Many of the leaders you engage with express feelings of isolation as a result of the constant change and unpredictability in their situations. Part of their sense of isolation stems from an underlying notion that they must solve all of their problems on their own. Your natural instinct is to increase your attention and individual efforts as the complexity and volume of your tasks grow. This can be a successful method when dealing with relatively short-term difficulties with well-known answers. It may be disastrous, however, when faced with difficulties when the whole scale of issues and interdependencies, let alone solutions, is unknown. Instead, now is the time to create the habit of purposefully reaching out to your network and beyond for advice and information. The difficulty is that, despite the effort put out by business executives, most attempts to make organizations adaptive fail. The author's personal experience working in management and as a strategy consultant supports this. When you ask senior executives what went wrong, you'll hear the same concerns again and over: Some employees inside the company neglected to accept responsibility for the transition process. People began blaming one another. Nothing was done about it when things went wrong. The metamorphosis slowed down over time.

For many flexible firms, profit plans have been replaced by promises of company continuity. Many businesses put long-term aspirations on hold to meet the needs of a workforce concerned about their future, stakeholders facing unpredictable demands, and operational obstacles. The challenge of labor planning is mitigated to some extent in industries where remote employment is available. However, it will necessitate more unlearning and upskilling. While some businesses balked at the new expectations owing to a lack of digital preparedness, purpose-driven businesses maintained spirits high and order volumes high by delivering online.

The issue is that tighter restrictions may suffocate an organization. In truth, management should relinquish control and allow the business the flexibility it requires to function efficiently. The concept is that management should focus on stating their goals and letting the company figure out how to get there. It might be difficult to let go of your grasp while not allowing the firm to fall apart. It must be founded on a defined set of concepts that are supported by science.

Adaptive challenges require new learning and can only be addressed by changing people's assumptions, beliefs, habits, and allegiances. Technical problems can be very complex and important, but the solutions are known and can be solved by deploying already available expertise, processes, and operating procedures, such as a medical problem solved by surgery. Expertise and prior knowledge can aid in the resolution of adaptive challenges, but the most important task is to mobilize and guide individuals through a time of discovery that leads to a revitalized ability to thrive. Culture shifts after mergers or societal revolutions such as civil rights are examples.

Adaptability to shifting situations is a must-have attribute for firms in today's unpredictable environment. Businesses may learn from nature's transformation playbook to become more flexible in an increasingly complex and unpredictable world. It is becoming increasingly obvious that all species' ability to recognize change and promptly adapt to it is more crucial than ever. Businesses may learn how to survive and prosper in the face of increasing change and unpredictability by looking to nature for inspiration. The underlying purpose of the individuals in these systems—creatures and enterprises alike—is to survive. This is one of the most striking parallels between nature and business.

Business leaders must prioritize flexibility as a must-have organizational attribute if they want to position themselves for long-term success in this changing climate. Traditional metrics of business health are no longer sufficient. To become adaptive now and survive tomorrow, they must shift their mindset and transform swiftly and at scale, but how? Many corporate executives continue to assume that conventional market dominance indicators give an unbeatable competitive edge. However, data shows that when disruption intensifies, the largest and "strongest" business firms are not always the most likely to survive. As the epidemic has progressed, this has become increasingly obvious, with many businesses, large and small, trying to cope with the COVID-19 disruption and its consequences.

For every firm, transformation simply means continuous progress. You, like sharks, must keep swimming in order to survive. The world changes all the time; customers' issued statements shift, risk profiles shift, and business models shift. As a result, you must change to stay up with the times. Survival is more important than transformation. That has been our strategy since the beginning. Transformation has not been simple and will continue to be difficult. In today's ever-changing business market, you must remain relevant and take aggressive initiatives to ensure that you stay ahead of the curve.

However, the transformation does not produce instant, demonstrable results, especially in the face of increased company expenses and the introduction of several identical items, disturbing market equilibriums. Workforce transformation is required for company change to be successful. Existing employees needed to be retrained, and new employees with strong technical and engineering backgrounds needed to be recruited to help with the change. Businesses that do not change and adapt may not be able to survive in the long run. Business owners are forced to explore how to pivot their business models for the future.

Finding the appropriate combination of challenge and support is the art of leader development.

In today's extremely dynamic climate, thriving, and possibly even surviving, demands ongoing, future-focused work that allows you to prepare and react to the change and uncertainty that lie ahead. Businesses that are proactive and strategic in managing their adaptive efforts will be the most successful. This entails adapting your business to changes in your ecosystem as well as adopting opportunities within the ecosystem to assist your firm in changing for the better. The speed of change in today's business climate is faster than it has ever been, as practically every business book now published will tell you. However, this has been the case for decades. The present environment has been more dynamic than ever before for a long time.

The most difficult problem is changing people's attitudes. The majority of people dislike change. My most difficult task was persuading people who did not realize you needed to adapt even more quickly. I collected everyone who was excited about our transition and turned them into internal champions to help rouse the troops. Another problem is determining the proper technology and making the choice to adopt it. The most recent technology may not be the best option because it is not always reliable and suitable for use in our clients' environments. As a result, evaluating the most appropriate security solutions for our clients must be done methodically, taking into account their risk assessment, budget, operational requirements and demands, as well as technology.

Adaptive leadership focuses on change that allows people, organizations, and society to grow or thrive. The most prevalent cause of failure is treating adaptive challenges as if they were technical issues. The majority of issues are a combination of technical and adaptive obstacles. In the corporate sector, for example, a merger will involve technical elements, but the adaptive parts pose a bigger risk since the newly merged enterprises will need to change their cultural norms, power structures, and value systems.

Businesses can no longer wait to investigate a market trend or new opportunity until the market – or a competitor – has proved that it is a safe path to take. By the time you notice that a business move is safe for the majority, it has already progressed to the point where your company is struggling to stay afloat. Following a corporate trend or hopping on a technical bandwagon, on the other hand, is rarely an appropriate approach. Worse, you risk causing unforeseen repercussions that will take years to correct. Importantly, most organizations adopt a risk-based approach to change, in which they only accept the presence of an issue or danger when it becomes a big problem or threat, showing itself as a bad economic performance outcome.

Reacting to change in this manner puts you at risk of falling behind in a race that penalizes those who can't keep up. They create outside-in and inside-out technology adaptations. It's all too tempting to get caught up in accepting technical change for the sake of embracing technological change—to adapt your company to the outside technological environment. However, the most successful firms adapt to emerging technology to meet their internal demands, such as strategic goals and operating environments. This results in two-way adaptation, with business direction being used to analyze the possible implications of changing business landscapes and adjustments in that landscape being used to decide the path of future company directions.

Loss, not change, is what people and human systems fight against. Adaptive problems are difficult to overcome since change always entails a sense of loss. Any change endeavor needs leadership with the capacity to diagnose what losses will be suffered. Adaptive change that works does not discard the past, but rather builds on it. Adaptive challenges aren't only about change; they're also about keeping things going. As a result, leaders must also determine the critical aspects that must be maintained. Diversity enhances the ability to adapt and occurs as a result of exploration.

People in organizations and politicians face similar challenges and pressures. However, it is anticipated that in public organizations such as legislatures, individuals will raise genuine concerns. In most other companies, this level of transparency is frowned upon. Adaptive leaders must understand the importance of politics and think in terms of politics. The idea is to recognize that your employees are working hard to satisfy the expectations of their numerous stakeholders and constituencies. Only until you grasp the nature of these expectations, as well as each stakeholder's potential to affect the situation, unique set of desires and requirements, and intended results, can you mobilize effectively. Adaptive leadership is all about finding a means to dissastify and disapoint people in order to mobilize them for the real work that has to be done. As an adaptable leader, you must be willing to upset the status quo and encourage people to go to new and unfamiliar locations that are potentially dangerous, unsettling, and confusing. Most businesses have minimal adaptive leadership behavior because adaptive leaders must risk speaking what has to be stated rather than what others desire to hear.

Organizations, like individuals, frequently have a misalignment between their espoused values and how they actually behave. According to research, the human brain reacts more to what a person does than to what they say they want to do. As a result, these behavioral patterns have become de facto organizational standards. When faced with competing commitments, those in positions of power must make judgments that result in losses for some and gains for others. Organizational leaders, on the other hand, frequently dodge these difficult decisions or try to find a solution that benefits no one. Adaptive leadership entails determining who and what groups will suffer losses, as well as the nature of those losses. There are usually two sorts of talk going on in an organizational setting: what individuals say out loud and what they are truly saying in their brains. The most crucial information in every conversation is almost never uttered aloud.

Utilize the expertise and experience of the people who are on the frontlines of delivering business value—servicing your customers, developing what you manufacture, or sustaining your day-to-day company operations—while you investigate technology advances. Then enlist the help of those who are most knowledgeable about the technology to see what's achievable. Rather than requiring businesses to adapt to new technologies, technology facilitates commercial value. Business transition has long been associated with the organization's strategy alterations. Business transformation is no longer an option in today's cause-and-effect society. Whether you like it or not, your company reacts to this changing dynamic. Your task is to steer that transformation in the right direction.Whether you like it or not, your company reacts to this changing dynamic. Your task is to take charge of that transformation and provide an opportunity to adjust to bad circumstances before they have a detrimental influence on you and your bottom line.

Power Points

- Every business leader understands that in order to thrive in the long run, their organization must adapt.
- Some employees inside the company neglected to accept responsibility for the transition process.
- Adaptive challenges require new learning and can only be addressed by changing people's assumptions, beliefs, habits, and allegiances.
- Organizations, like individuals, frequently have a misalignment between their espoused values and how they actually behave.
- Adaptive leaders must understand the importance of politics and think in terms of politics.

CHAPTER THREE

TRAITS & BEHAVIORS

Adaptive Leaders Recognize And Embrace Adversity.

"Before you are a leader, success is all about growing yourself. When you become a leader, success is all about growing others." —Jack Welch

As a company grows, it is inevitable that it will face uncertainty. Leaders who can assist staff through difficult periods and learn to solve recurring issues may have a significant influence on the process. That is why adaptive leadership is critical. Adaptive leadership is a management philosophy that aims to help businesses embrace change and uncertainty rather than merely handle them. This allows businesses to successfully adjust while maintaining their core principles and strengths. Change has taken on a three-dimensional form. It's all-encompassing, never-ending, and rapidly expanding. Leaders can no longer operate in a vacuum, making decisions and taking actions from the *"helm"* of a company. Leaders must adapt in order for organizations to succeed in today's atmosphere. The *"leader-as-hero"* style is no longer effective, and the alternative represents a transition toward more intelligent, collaborative leadership. Adaptive leadership is the term for this. In comparison to contemporary paradigms, it radiates more honesty, humility, and vulnerability.

Leaders with an adaptable style are performance-driven, self-aware, and have a high level of emotional intelligence. They delegate the appropriate responsibilities to the appropriate individuals and give resources for professional growth. While they do take decisive action, they almost never do it in a reactionary manner without taking into account all possible consequences. Because they establish dynamic teams that welcome change and channel anxiety into positive outcomes, adaptive leaders get better results. When your company is confronted with a technological transformation, a new client preference, or a new marketing dynamic such as the current economy, you must awaken the leader inside you to lead others through these changes. When your workload, team members, clients, and resources change on a regular basis, your leadership and management style must adapt as well.

Although the characteristic approach has been around for decades, there has been a rising focus on abilities that are particularly significant for adaptive leadership in recent years. These abilities include the capacity to comprehend the leadership position and the flexibility to modify methods or actions in response to changing circumstances. Although evidence for the effects of certain talents on effective leadership is still scarce, the amount of research has increased in recent years. A study in which measurements of leadership abilities and personality are connected with markers of leadership effectiveness and, in some cases, with leadership behavior is the most common research strategy.

J.K. Rowling's inspiring story of success unless you've been living under a rock, you've heard of the Harry Potter series. However, the author is rather certain that most of you haven't heard of J.K. Rowling. If you're wondering who she is, she's the lady behind the world's most successful bestseller series. This remarkable woman is motivating and extraordinary in every way. Rowling's triumph is one of the most exhilarating, but it wasn't always smooth sailing. Few people know what happened to her before she became famous. J.K. Rowling's success story It is stated that true success follows a series of setbacks. This is precisely what happened to Rowling. Her personal life was in disarray, making each day difficult for her.

On a train voyage from Manchester to London one lovely morning in 1990, she created the complete plot from an idea and began building the story of Harry Potter on that route. Unfortunately, her mother died later that year, putting a stop to her writing for a while. When she went to Portugal in 1992 to teach English as a foreign language, her life had other intentions. She met, married, and had a daughter with him. In 1993, she filed for divorce from her then-husband after a year of marriage. With three chapters of Harry Potter, she made the decision to go to Edinburgh, Scotland, with her baby daughter to be closer to her sister. Rowling was divorced, jobless, and a single mother of a child at the time, and it was the most trying time of her life. She struggled with acute depression, yet she persisted. She discovered the light at the end of the tunnel when life was dark and dreary, constantly pushing through the trials and tribulations life threw at her. Failure and rejection Rowling's life was defined in so many ways by the year 1995. The Harry Potter script was rejected by roughly 12 prominent periodicals, not one, two, or five. She had been broken, but she had not been vanquished. She continued to pursue more newspapers, and her efforts were rewarded. The book was accepted for publication by a tiny publishing firm, and only 1000 copies were printed. Things began to change soon after the book received significant accolades, including the Nestle Smarties Book Prize and the British Book Award for Children's Book of the Year. The book has been translated into 73 languages and has sold over 500 million copies worldwide as of 2013.

Not to mention that the novel was made into a film series, making it a billion-dollar franchise. Are there any takeaways for you all? J.K. Rowling's most important lesson is to keep trying, believing, and acting on your dreams. Whether it's to become a great business or to publish a novel, there's something for everyone.

According to the author of this book, business environments are always changing and must be addressed effectively. Adaptive leadership theory helps professionals anticipate and identify the fundamental causes of problems and discover long-term solutions. This necessitates leaders being more than merely commanding officers. Instead, they must be receptive to input, ready for change, and willing to reverse direction if required.

Steve Jobs, Elon Musk, Mark Zuckerberg, and Oprah Winfrey are just a few examples of outstanding men and women who became phenomenally wealthy by taking chances and working smart. Elon Musk is the ultimate risk-taker and entrepreneur. Elon Musk is one of the few entrepreneurs who have never played it safe. He's been taking chances since the beginning. Some people were unsuccessful, while others were fortunate enough to win the lottery. To take on eBay, he joined with a rival and renamed the new business PayPal, which completely transformed the world of electronic payments. Musk was the largest stakeholder and walked away with $180 million when eBay purchased PayPal for $1.5 billion shortly after.

It's critical to use adaptable leadership to overcome problems. It's critical to understand the distinction between a technical and an adaptive problem while using adaptive leadership to overcome obstacles. A single-time solution can solve a technological problem completely. Adaptive difficulties are time-consuming and may necessitate organizational culture adjustments. They frequently occur during periods of expansion or transition, and they entail everyone in the company changing their long-term plans. Adaptive leadership's proactive character necessitates the recognition that some of the organization's existing business processes are unproductive. Adaptive leaders have a set of characteristics that they constantly display. Any person in the company may be a leader under an adaptive leadership model, and these attributes can be cultivated over time.

Every adaptive leader should have the following characteristics:

- The ability to link organizational change to the primary values, abilities, and dreams of the stakeholders involved.
- The ability to create an environment that embraces diversity of viewpoints and uses such collective knowledge to benefit the organization.
- The adaptable leader recognizes that change is a difficult process. As a result, he or she can anticipate and counteract any hesitant conduct on the part of colleagues.

- An knowledge that large-scale change is a slow process that needs perseverance and the fortitude to face the pressure that comes with it.
- Being proactive in seeking out possibilities and devoting the resources necessary to pursue them. Admitting when they've made a mistake and altering or discarding ineffective techniques.
- Being willing to try new things and take risks. Employees like and are encouraged to innovate.

- Adaptive leadership isn't about having a lot of power. It's about developing a feeling of organizational accountability in the whole workforce. Leadership is a shared responsibility. Leadership cannot always be the responsibility of one person in a world of constant and volatile change.
- Adaptive leaders develop personnel who can foresee what will happen, prepare for it, adjust to it, recover from setbacks, and keep going even when things are difficult.
- Adaptive leaders instill a feeling of common purpose in their teams and govern by influence rather than by command and control.
- Adaptive leadership necessitates new talents and competences, such as spirit, guts, heart, and mind. It takes guts to present your complete self to the conversation.
- Adaptive leaders encourage teams to generate outcomes by empowering people, and they give lots of praise and celebration for the team's achievement. They share the limelight with the squad and ensure that they get lots of favorable press for their work.

- Adaptive leaders are open to change and embrace it. It's the truth for them. They form dynamic teams that welcome change and use cooperation and communication to transform any uncertainty into great outcomes.
- Adaptive leaders make sure their staff are knowledgeable about the company's strategy and the context in which they operate, and then they step aside. Rather than checking in on their teammates, they check in. They also provide employees the freedom to work through concerns and solve problems.
- The adaptive leader must demonstrate resilience on a daily basis so that the capacity to handle adversity, remain cheerful and hopeful, and respond calmly to difficult events pervades the business.
- Emotional intelligence is a trait shared by adaptive leaders. As a result, they can immediately determine how an employee feels about a certain circumstance. In this part of the adaptive leadership paradigm, the affiliate leadership style might be effective. Once the leader understands the emotions at play, he or she can give the appropriate support so that this individual may continue to perform at their best. This, of course, necessitates a great deal of empathy on the part of the leader.
- Adaptive leaders have a set of characteristics that they constantly display. Any person in the company may be a leader under an adaptive leadership model, and these attributes can be cultivated over time. The characteristics of a good adaptable leader include the following:
- Adaptive leaders connect long-term corporate objectives to systematic transformation.Action is

conducted with the goal of achieving a certain outcome in mind.

- Adaptive leaders foster a progressive and open-minded work environment. Errors are recognized as a necessary part of the process.
- Adaptive leaders recognize and embrace adversity. They get their team members ready to solve problems. Adaptive leaders recognize that finding a long-term solution may take a few tries.
- Adaptive leaders understand that change takes time and are willing to put in the time required to build a better organization.
- Adaptive leaders are proactive in their approach. They detect problems and spend whatever resources are required to remedy them ahead of time.
- Adaptive leaders state their intentions openly and then let the participants play the game. The participants will either win or lose the game in the end.
- Adaptive leaders value relationships as much as they value money. This knowledge aids them in ensuring that organizational members and other stakeholders are on board with any long-term changes.
- Adaptive leadership may be summarized using four basic principles: dispersed leadership, appropriate talent mix, transparent character, and development. When it comes to dispersed leadership, the leader assigns duties to members of the team.
- Adaptive leaders are at ease with the unknown. They understand that not having a quick solution to an issue is an important element of the positive transformation process.

- Adaptive leaders enjoy experimenting with new ideas and solving problems.They are ready to evaluate their work and make adjustments as needed. They recognize that handling nebulous and difficult topics necessitates trial and error.

Flexible and adaptable leadership entails altering behavior in response to changing circumstances. Leaders who can effectively evaluate a situation and adjust their conduct accordingly have been referred to by a number of words. Flexible, adaptable, agile, and versatile are examples of these adjectives. There is still a lot of misunderstanding in management and leadership literature regarding what flexible leadership is and how to evaluate it. Flexible leadership may occur in a variety of situations, which adds to the uncertainty. For example, when situations change for a leader, flexibility is essential, as is flexibility when transferring from one sort of leadership role to another with different duties and tasks.

Behavioral flexibility and adaptability may be characterized and quantified in a variety of ways, with the signs varying depending on the circumstance. The degree to which a leader employs a range of diverse behaviors is one sign. To be adaptable, however, the chosen behaviors must be appropriate for the conditions in which they are utilized. As a result, the extent to which a leader's conduct varies in ways that are acceptable for different tasks and subordinates is a stronger predictor of flexibility. In a normal day or week, most leaders are responsible for a variety of duties, and it is sometimes required to move swiftly from one sort of work to another. Different jobs typically necessitate different leadership styles. Furthermore, because subordinates differ in terms of experience, talents, beliefs, and requirements, a leader's conduct with various individuals should vary. For subordinates with good talents and a strong dedication to work objectives, for example, increased delegation is suitable. When a subordinate's talents and motivations vary over time, flexibility is also essential. Using the same scenario, greater delegation will be acceptable as a subordinate acquires experience and confidence.

It is never a good idea to give up. Agree?

Walt Disney didn't have an easy life. Because quitting was never an option for Walt Disney, a guy of action, determination, aspirations, and passion, he altered the world of entertainment and animation. Do you know that Walt Disney was once fired from a newspaper for being too creative? His first animation firm, however, was a flop. His theme park concept was turned down. His first several animated flicks failed miserably. If he had been going through a bad patch, Walt would have become one of those homeless men yelling about his failure. He didn't give up, though. Now you're all talking about his success. His animation company became the most well-known in the world, and Disney Land and Disney World are two of the most popular and profitable theme parks in the world.

Many successful people have gone through the same thing, and you're talking about them now. So reconsider! What do you do when you're on the verge of giving up? Are you afraid of taking risks? Learn how to be a great performer. You must take chances regardless of whether you are a risk taker or not. To be honest, you may have taken a few chances to get to where you are now, and you will continue to do so in the future. Then why not go all-in and do things that terrify the very daylights out of us? What makes you fearful of taking risks? Risk is defined as the possibility of losing anything significant, such as money, a job, one's health, a relationship, or anything else that is precious or dear to you.

The capacity to grasp the leadership situation, including political processes and social interactions, as well as the ability to pick an acceptable reaction and alter one's conduct in response to changing situations, is referred to as social intelligence. Empathy, self-awareness, and the capacity to control one's own emotions are all examples of emotional intelligence. Empathy for others' sentiments is critical when deciding how to influence and motivate them. The capacity to recognize your own ideals, intentions, and effectiveness in influencing others is referred to as self-awareness. Self-control of emotions entails the capacity to avoid mood swings and emotional reactions that obstruct problem solutions, such as panic during a crisis.

One of the big five personality qualities is openness to learning and new ideas, which is critical for leaders who must adapt to changing circumstances. This characteristic involves the capacity to take feedback regarding the influence of your actions on others. A person who depends on habitual patterns of conduct while ignoring negative feedback or fresh ideas is unlikely to be adaptable and flexible. Success in higher-level employment is predicted by the capacity to learn from experience. Feedback from many sources (e.g., subordinates, peers, employers, clients) may help a leader become more aware of key qualities, abilities, and behaviors, and coaching is vital for leaders who must adapt to changing situations.

Adaptive leadership, as suggested by the author, poses a number of difficulties. Experimenting, learning new information, and making multiple modifications throughout your firm are all part of this leadership paradigm. You will only be able to maintain the changes and prosper if you modify your mindset and adjust your policies. Changing people's attitudes, beliefs, and perceptions, on the other hand, is frequently more difficult than flossing a cat's teeth.

Making adjustments necessitates a degree of disloyalty to your past. If you wish to execute a new marketing strategy, for example, you must first accept that your existing marketing methods are unsuccessful. Most top executives are hesitant to abandon long-standing rules that helped their firms get off the ground. Sticking to old habits, on the other hand, might prevent you from reaping the benefits of new tactics. Another issue with adaptive leadership is that it creates an environment conducive to various types of opposition. This might be from your employees or other stakeholders in the organization. Stakeholder Any individual, group, or entity with an interest in an organization and the effects of its activities is referred to as a stakeholder in business.

Marginalizing, distracting, and assaulting are the most prevalent techniques used to stymie adaptive change. If you see any of these behaviors, it's likely that your staff are resisting the new policy you're attempting to impose. The refusal of leaders to listen to other people's perspectives is perhaps the biggest obstacle posed by adaptive leadership. Adaptive leadership, as previously said, is more about cooperation than it is about power. Adaptive leaders, in principle, should be open to listening to and modifying suggestions made by coworkers or clients.

In actuality, only a small number of leaders are prepared to listen to others who disagree with them. What such leaders fail to realize is that listening does not always imply forsaking one's own objectives. It simply implies that you have a better understanding of your employees' requirements. As a result, you'll be able to work more efficiently to implement modifications. Although adaptive leadership demands a significant amount of work, it pays off handsomely. Adaptive businesses, according to trustworthy statistics, reap enormous financial and operational benefits. Even during moments of turbulence, they are able to withstand storms and surge to the top.

Examining the issue to determine which obstacles are technical and which are adaptive Leaders must manage emotionally charged circumstances based on opposing values, beliefs, and loyalties while scoping. Experts and traditional problem-solving approaches have repeatedly attempted but failed to address the problem, which is a telltale indicator of adaptive difficulties.

Diagnose the environment in order to identify and comprehend people, processes, and technological systems and subsystems that maintain the status quo and the factions that profit from and protect the status quo. This involves learning about cultural norms, traditions, and rituals in a certain setting. The environment must be diagnosed before the adaptation challenge can be diagnosed. Diagnoses come before cures, just as they do in medicine.

The author expert in adaptive leadership, says that leaders who understand and support flexibility have a distinct perspective on their employees. They encourage everyone in the company to take on a leadership position. Adaptive leaders aim to create a working culture where informal leaders throughout the business are innovating and pushing change from the bottom up, rather than the conventional position where the leader takes the choices and they are pushed down from the top. However, encouraging employees at all levels to take responsibility rather than expecting to be given solutions and told what to do may be a significant cultural adjustment for many businesses.

This unique, world-class, cutting-edge approach to how a company operates does not arise by chance. According to the author , an organization's senior leadership should ask, *"What are our values and how do we live them?" "How do they appear at different levels of the organization?"* Then there should be open and honest discussions with middle management, as well as input from them. Employees must also be included when you explain this new way of thinking and determine whether they are interested in taking on a larger role. This is in stark contrast to what can occur, for instance, at a yearly performance review, while assessing someone's progress. That discussion might be about a certain degree, course, or goal that someone is pursuing.

It's a more comprehensive view of each individual in adaptive leadership than just their job description. *"These are the strengths I see in you, and here's how we'd want to leverage them so you can shine here,"* you say to the individual. Here are the flaws you see and to help you in those areas, the author would want to place you in a safe atmosphere where you can work on them and see if you can get better at them with a little practice. You are better prepared for the difficulties and changes ahead when you draw on your particular talents, abilities, and expertise. Workers at all levels are happy because they have the opportunity to advance, lead, and shine. In essence, an adaptable leader recognizes and capitalizes on an employee's individuality. Identifying a person's flaws and assisting them in improving them, or accepting that not everyone is competent at everything.

As a result, adaptive leadership nearly always requires you to analyze, manage, distribute, and provide context for losses in order to move people to a new location. Answering concerns concerning adaptive change and the losses it entails is challenging in any case because it necessitates difficult decisions, trade-offs, and the uncertainty of continual experimental trial and error. That is a difficult job not only because it is academically challenging, but also because it tests people and organizations' commitment to connections, competence, and identity. It necessitates a change in the tales they've told themselves and the rest of the world about what they believe in, stand for, and represent.

Adaptive leadership is the discipline of organizing individuals to face and overcome difficult circumstances. The notion that you need to reform organizations because they are *"dysfunctional"* is a misconception. In actuality, human systems work the way they do because the people who live in them want them to. When you realize this, you'll change the way you approach the situation. If you realize that a seemingly dysfunctional organization is actually operating for many of its members, then you'll use a variety of strategies and approaches. Rather than trying to persuade people that your image of the organization is correct, you'll learn to focus on how to motivate and support them through a hazardous and terrifying transformation.

Adaptive leaders must be able to self-manage in the face of uncertainty, as well as assist others in dealing with their own discomfort. When you ask people and organizations challenging questions and ask them to be accountable for matters that are outside the scope of their professions, they feel disequilibrium. The temperature of a productive disequilibrium is continually managed by an adaptable leader. Only by staying in this productive zone are teams and organizations able to deal with complex adaptation difficulties.

Power Points

- Adaptive difficulties are time-consuming and may necessitate organizational culture adjustments.
- Adaptive leadership necessitates new talents and competences, such as spirit, guts, heart, and mind.
- Adaptive leadership is the discipline of organizing individuals to face and overcome difficult circumstances.
- Adaptive leaders foster a progressive and open-minded work environment.
- Strategic leadership requires cognitive skills, which are more critical at higher levels of management, as previously stated.

CHAPTER FOUR

QUALITIES & APPLICATIONS

Adaptability And Constant Innovation Are Essential For Survival.

"You can't build an adaptable organization without adaptable people--and individuals change only when they have to, or when they want to." -Gary Hamel

There are various paradigms and definitions of leadership agility. The paradigm of one distinctive leadership style is slipping away in current times, and each scenario will require a different sort of leader. The team's agility is becoming increasingly important. As a result, leadership agility is built on an agile team that can pivot in a new direction as the situation requires. Adaptive leaders strike a compromise between their ideal vision of what they want to achieve and the realities of their lives and schedules.

A successful strategy in a digital environment necessitates critical decisions about which markets to pursue and what products or services are required to win. However, outer-game concerns should not eclipse the inner-game imperatives of developing a data-driven and adaptable company model. After all, a flexible organization ensures that businesses allocate the appropriate people and resources to their most critical opportunities. During the epidemic, one of the most important lessons learned was that every company must learn to anticipate and manage change and unpredictability. You've all heard it before: the speed of change has never been quicker, and it's not going to slow down anytime soon. And technology CEOs are frequently at the forefront of change.

Adaptive leaders are always looking for new methods to match pivotal events with shifting consumer preferences. They are attempting to alter client preferences in ways that benefit both their companies and their customers. They train their employees for both expected and unexpected outcomes. They can feel when things are about to change and react rapidly. These adaptable leaders do a great job of operating and adapting.

"Become the kind of leader that people would follow voluntarily; even if you had no title or position." —Brian Tracy

Curiosity encourages executives to ask questions to better understand how new knowledge affects their company, customers, and people. It's a critical component of effective leadership. Leaders must avoid becoming overly enamored with a particular plan or strategy, as the pace of change in today's environment is only increasing. Adaptable leaders will be prepared with Plan B (and C). In times of transition, leaders shouldn't feel compelled to go it alone; instead, they should enlist the help of mentors, friends, coaches, trusted peers, professional colleagues, family members, and others. When you understand your own reactions to change and can better manage your emotions and reactions, your ability to adapt improves. Reframe dangerous situations as chances to learn and develop. You may use this when you're presented with change, but you can also practice this by embracing new experiences on a regular basis. Adaptability takes time to develop, but by taking action, leaders may become more flexible and effective, which will benefit themselves, their teams, and their businesses.

Businesses are facilitated by changing organizational structures. Adaptive companies aren't scared to embrace possibilities that aren't directly related to their core business. Adaptive IT executives strive to include flexibility in their business structures. Consistency, scalability, and adaptability are provided by platform teams. High-performing companies organize themselves around the work that needs to be done, relying on partner ecosystems to unbundle work while simultaneously driving innovation. At the onset of the pandemic, a customized business goods firm saw a new potential in the marketplace to make masks and collaborated with partners to swiftly offer what would become one of the most popular products.

These adaptable leaders are able to function effectively, adapt rapidly, invent new methods of working, and alter their businesses in a seamless manner. Because they are so absorbed in their difficulties, leaders frequently become trapped. *"Zooming out,"* or moving from *"the dance floor to the balcony,"* as Ron Heifetz, Marty Linksy, and Alexander Grashow describe it in The Practice of Adaptive Leadership, gives you a broader perspective and a systemic view of the issues, and can reveal unexamined assumptions that would otherwise go undetected. Interdependencies and wider patterns become visible from this *"balcony"* or elevated vantage point, possibly revealing unanticipated difficulties and new solutions. This more comprehensive viewpoint allows for better adaptability and, when necessary, path adjustment. By making this dance floor-balcony change a regular practice, you may increase your capacity to perceive the larger picture and grow as a leader.

Organizations must produce leaders who can adjust themselves and their organizations to deal with challenges now. Development of adaptive leadership a new leadership development framework is required. One that can be given at scale and creates adaptable leaders at all levels, sooner in their careers and in the flow of their work. The new model stresses learning in the context of the organization's business conditions, processes, and objectives, as well as quick implementation of what has been learned. Implementing adaptive leadership poses a number of challenges. Even while adaptive leadership is a valuable theory, putting it into practice may be difficult. There are two key hurdles that a leader must overcome while attempting to adopt this framework:One of the most significant challenges for an adaptable leader is the human instinct to resist change.

Authority figures have an impact on people. If you don't model the act of naming sensitive topics as the authority, it's doubtful that anybody else would. Your job is to keep them safe and encourage them to speak up. When they say anything that makes you uncomfortable, be interested and encourage them to elaborate on their notions. People feel a sense of shared responsibility for the overall organization when: people offer to provide resources to help others; rewards are based at least partially on the overall organization's performance; new ideas and insights are shared across boundaries; and people take the time to understand what others are doing in other areas of the organization. Some authority figures value independence because it provides them with a sense of importance. The adaptable leader's task is to become expendable by continually delegating work to others. Adaptive leadership fosters a culture of leadership across the company.

Adaptive leaders have strong personalities and adhere to a system of ethics and beliefs. Adaptive leaders are good at generating trust, which is necessary for implementing successful solutions to adaptive difficulties. They hold themselves to the same standards that they hold others to, resulting in a culture of openness and respect. So far, you've looked at what adaptive leadership is, why it's essential, and some of the concepts that underpin it. Let's take a look at a few talents that an adaptable leader must possess.

- Leadership that can adapt who accept that uncertainty is an unavoidable aspect of change and are content not to have all of the answers all of the time.
- They emphasize experimenting and learning as a means of arriving at the best possible answers to a challenge.
- They are emotionally aware and do not allow personal sentiments to come in the way of making good judgments for the company.
- They place a high value on relationships and devote time to establishing trust and hearing diverse points of view that differ from their own.
- They recognize that change takes time and might be unpleasant.
- They are patient and persistent till they achieve their goals.
- They foster a feeling of shared purpose and values among employees so that they may make independent,

self-directed decisions that are in line with the company's aims and strategy.

The adaptive leadership philosophy emphasizes overcoming obstacles in order to achieve organizational success. This entails assisting stakeholders in navigating new and complex circumstances that arise as a result of improvement activities. When tackling any situational problem linked with a change attempt, leaders who try to take an adaptable approach should consider the following characteristics, as the author explains in his book on adaptive leadership.

- The desired speed of change will not be achieved by the organic evolution of the tech stack. Adaptive businesses make use of technology platforms and ecosystem partners to boost their ability to offer consumer value faster. Adaptive businesses make use of technology platforms and ecosystem partners to boost their capacity to offer customer value at scale by using thin customisation layers. Platforms help innovation chains expedite the adoption of new technologies and capabilities. A major insurance firm developed many basic technology platforms, reducing time-to-market by 21% and increasing efficiency by 19%.
- Firms cannot afford to wait for trends to emerge before acting. Adaptive businesses use data to foresee and respond to growing client demands and expectations. Adaptive businesses strive to build virtuous cycles in which they can use consumer and partner information to continuously give value and spot emerging requirements. A prominent industrial manufacturing business has embedded digital capabilities into its

products to increase performance, do predictive maintenance, and establish a stronger relationship and greater value for its customers.

- To allow change, you must be able to persuade others to say *"yes"* to your demands. You may reduce opposition by presenting your request as a solution that supports the stakeholders' vision. Being a controversial person whose requests don't regard their stakeholders is a rapid road to failure and alienation. The aim is to pique people's interest in talking about your request so you may express your ideas. If your stakeholders, on the other hand, appear indifferent, leave it alone until the dialogue and the right opportunity arise again.

- Execute each duty according to the roles, duties, and instructions you've been given until you've earned the right to speak for others. As you earn the ability to advocate on your own behalf, be sure your actions are always in line with the purpose, vision, and objectives of those who are empowering you. Being intrapreneurial is a great way to start a business. The capacity to deliver quick, succinct, and insightful ideas to stakeholders is critical for a powerful leader's day-to-day. The manner in which you participate also influences the future possibilities for you to be welcomed. Nonetheless, your capacity to express and convince people in your business with authority is critical to your success.

- Although competent leaders are more comfortable making partial judgements and discovering gray areas within doctrine in order to achieve their goals in the near term, they nevertheless rely on chain of command direction for all of their decisions. Adaptive leaders, on the other hand, are similar to intrapreneurs in that they see operational possibilities and create visions to profit from them.

- To respond to opportunities and disruptions, cross-functional teams must adjust all organizational systems, including incentives and recognition, talent management, and learning and development. Begin with your own personal knowledge and abilities. When you've found adaptable leaders, search for leadership, technology, and management knowledge from outside sources to continue expanding your adaptive leadership schema. To help you scale, create a leadership team with a single leadership system attitude. Integrate organizational leadership competence and capacity into leaders' daily work flows. Integrate critical thinking, diversity, and other behavioral skills into the content and learning experience.

- A diverse attitude adaptive leadership is based on a diversity-welcoming worldview. This is not the narrow concept of diversity that frequently leads to tokenism, whether perceived or real. Real diversity tests established ways of thinking and working, and it pervades various aspects of a company, including three main areas: To begin, promoting the advancement of diverse people entails not just recruiting and promoting individuals of other colors or genders, but also those who think differently and challenge established standards. Second, more personalized career advancement rather than a set, standard, and linear career ladder allows for more different career pathways. Third, recruiting, onboarding, learning and development, and performance management procedures should all include the delivery of intended results.

As previously said, change frequently necessitates many stakeholders letting go of what they consider valuable or familiar. Beliefs, values, actions, identities, and ideologies may all change as a result of this. Changing any of these factors might be difficult. Adaptive leaders must set their egos aside and be open to letting go of their own ideas, taking responsibility for their mistakes, and delegating power and authority in order to find the greatest possible answer to the adaptive situation at hand. For leaders, overcoming these internal struggles may be a big task.

What are some examples of how adaptive leaders approach to solve a problem?

Let's take a look at a few instances of organizational issues and how an adaptable leader could handle the situation. You worked in a team managed by a well-respected and admired leader a few years back. Your leader was capable, ethical, and humble, and he really cared about his people. He chose to quit the organization due to a change in his circumstances, which disappointed practically everyone on his team. He was replaced by a new boss who had been hired from outside the company. There was a lot of concern about the incoming leader and how this changeover would affect all of your lives. The new leader might have stepped in and acted from a position of power. He might have viewed the move as a technical issue, with all he needed to do now being to ensure that the knowledge transfer was complete and that he was prepared to handle the business's operations. However, he knew that this method would almost certainly lead to problems down the road because he required his team's buy-in to succeed. As a result, he chose an adaptable approach, first accepting that the shift would be difficult for the squad and that he would be filling enormous shoes.

Developing a leadership pipeline is critical for the organization's long-term flexibility. When self-organizing, cross-functional teams become the rule rather than the exception, innovation thrives. Top innovators create a flexible organizational structure that allows employees across the company to align themselves with new innovation initiatives that excite them. A flexible organization necessitates new working methods. While firms have typically relied on gut feelings and manager discretion when making crucial personnel choices, digital leaders are increasingly turning to behavioral analytics. The goal here isn't to peek over individual employees' shoulders, but rather to examine behavior patterns to see if they match the strategic aim. This kind of knowledge may lead to significant improvements in recruiting, training, incentives, and team coordination.

Early in 2021, Forrester forecasted that a fifth of the Fortune 500's tech-laggard firms would fail to make it through the year. Those businesses that are able to take advantage of the market's dynamism will prosper in this climate. According to Forrester, companies that have a future-fit strategy are able to restructure their basic business principles to produce and deliver in this new world. According to Forrester, companies that have a future-fit strategy are better prepared to rearrange their basic business principles to generate and deliver value to fulfill consumer expectations in this new world. And the distinction is striking. According to a Forrester assessment of prominent companies, adaptable companies grew roughly three times faster than the industry average. Future-ready leaders do this by employing adaptable technology, making decisions based on predictive insights, and creating a flexible organization that can react to changing market conditions.

Adaptive leadership is the deliberate evolution of a leader in real time, sometimes under difficult conditions. It will motivate you to challenge—and perhaps reject—the current quo in favor of innovative approaches. It will almost certainly be necessary to change attitudes and views, as well as to combat hesitant conduct. What steps can you take to become a more adaptable leader? According to the importance of emotional intelligence, the five competences of emotional intelligence are self-awareness, self-management, social awareness, empathy, and social relationship management. To succeed in positions of power, you'll need these abilities. Adaptive leaders also make fair judgments, share knowledge, retain integrity, develop others, and continue to grow throughout their lives. Adaptive challenges are problems that experts are unable to solve. They necessitate in-house tests, findings, and changes. People must accept new values and attitudes, as well as absorb the change, in order to make the adaptive jump. Adaptive leaders lead with empathy, learn from their mistakes, accept change, and create conditions that benefit the greatest number of people. Adaptive leadership may help authority figures see the broad picture and delegate important work back to individuals and teams during times of crisis.

Many changes entail adaptation issues that require people to develop new skills. In corporate and community transformation attempts, this is frequently disregarded. People must adapt to address challenges in order for the shift to be effective. Adapt or change is required of both leaders and individuals. Individuals must develop their own capacity to solve issues and capitalize on opportunities. Many of your greater societal crises, such as climate change, do not have a technology solution to transition from individual to systemic challenges. You need people to modify what they do until there is a technological answer, and you need to address the bigger adaptive issues involved in making these adjustments, which include, among other things, value systems and identity. Leaders must mobilize their followers to modify existing habits and build new ones.

It's easy to simplify difficult problems to make them appear less intimidating. Breaking down a difficulty into its constituent parts, for example, might make you feel more in control of the situation, but it can also restrict your perspective and mask important interdependencies, giving you a false feeling of security. Drawing comparisons from previous issues might be valuable, but it can also lead to you overlooking the particular details of the current challenge. Leaders must learn to combine their drive for action with a disciplined approach to comprehending both the fundamental problem and their own biases, rather than succumbing to the need for speedy solutions. Adaptive leaders know how to invent alternate uses of things to promote their vision, just as core and effective leaders know how to identify what should and shouldn't work. Core leadership, the author feels, equals book smarts, successful leadership equals street smarts, and adaptable leadership means inventiveness. To put it another way, core leaders are recognized for their competency, successful leaders for their expertise, and adaptable leaders for their visions with flexible paths. The greater the level of uncertainty, the more untrainable leadership development is infused.

Adaptive leadership promotes creativity, progress, and positive reactions to change. Learn about the characteristics of adaptable leadership and how to use it in difficult situations. environments that are difficult to work in. You have recently been chosen to lead a firm that has had a slew of issues in the past. The business is in financial trouble, but the environment is also an issue. Employees have little faith in the company's leadership. There is a lot of tension in the corporate world between different groups, including politics, gender, ethnicity, and other concerns. You are both delighted and anxious. How can you possibly be the leader in such a difficult situation? Many company problems are presented in terms of income, but the fact is that many business problems stem from unsolved difficulties in a difficult work environment. This might indicate a problem with polarization in politics or prejudice. It might also refer to situations where different groups believe in conflicting visions for the organization or when there is a lot of distrust and unhappiness. Let's look at adaptable leadership and tactics for execution in a demanding environment to help you think about how to manage your team.

Power Points

- Development of adaptive leadership a new leadership development framework is required.
- One of the most significant challenges for an adaptable leader is the human instinct to resist change.
- Adaptive leadership fosters a culture of leadership across the company.
- Developing a leadership pipeline is critical for the organization's long-term flexibility.
- Adaptive leadership promotes creativity, progress, and positive reactions to change.

CHAPTER FIVE

COMPETENCY BUILDING

Adaptive Leaders Aren't Afraid Of Failure.

"Leadership is lifting a person's vision to high sights, the raising of a person's performance to a higher standard, the building of a personality beyond its normal limitations."
—Peter Drucker

Adaptive leaders and their teams become more resilient as a result of their adaptability. They get stronger as a result of their blunders. Leaders who keep going and endure in the face of adversity attain success. When they stop trying, they call it *"failure."* Adaptive leaders allow everyone to make mistakes. It will re-energize a company.

"I have not failed," Thomas Edison is reported as saying. I've come up with 10,000 methods that won't work. "

Development of adaptive leadership a new leadership development framework is required. One that can be given at scale and creates adaptable leaders at all levels, sooner in their careers and in the flow of their work. The new model stresses learning in the context of the organization's business conditions, processes, and objectives, as well as quick implementation of what has been learned. Starting with helping leaders understand the business, including its goals, mission, and goods and services, there are multiple activities and numerous keys to producing adaptable leaders.

Adaptive ability will continue to determine who emerges on top and who goes away in 2022. HR executives can assist corporate leaders in evaluating their default habits and embracing their ability to adjust. The epidemic shook up the corporate world, especially in terms of how people see leadership, delegation, performance management, and trust. It also prompted concerns regarding remote work productivity, procedures that obstruct existing processes, new health and safety-related job standards, and how to benefit from new production and delivery methods. The ability of businesses to respond to these issues is strongly tied to their executives' ability to adapt.

Take a step back and consider the overall difficulty of the situation. To gain perspective and understand the larger picture, an adaptable leader must switch between being an observer and being a participant. Assess the situation to determine whether the challenge is technical or adaptive in nature. Adaptive difficulties are complicated, fluid, and alter with conditions, whereas technical challenges may be handled by an expert's expertise. If the problem is adaptable, the leader should collaborate with stakeholders to overcome it using calculative steps. Leaders must always provide coherence to a continuous improvement process by buffering it from—or linking it to—other imperatives that exist in a district at any given time if it is to thrive. Leaders will encounter conflicting expectations without any buffering or bridging, making it impossible to produce anything cohesive.

Adaptive leaders aren't afraid of failure. You pay close attention to the effort required to navigate the adaptive difficulty. Many people will try to resist change since it forces them to labor outside of their comfort zone. Ignoring the difficulty, blaming others, or diverting one's efforts are all examples of avoidance behaviors. Instead of avoiding the problem, an adaptable leader assists stakeholders in confronting it head-on. When negotiating the adaptive hurdles connected with school reform initiatives, it's crucial to remember that these adaptive leadership typically occur concurrently and interdependently.

Adaptive leaders create environments that encourage experimentation, learning, and reflection on both success and failure. Failure is viewed as a learning opportunity by adaptive leaders, and experimentation is praised even if the desired objective is not reached. The important thing is to keep going ahead. It's critical to figure out why something failed quickly and then move on. If they aren't making errors, the adaptive leader believes they aren't working hard enough. Successful corporations that accept failure are Netflix, Amazon, and Coca-Cola. You can't learn unless you fail, and you can't achieve until you face obstacles. Traditional leadership training methods appear to take individuals as they are and turn them into leaders by talking to them about leadership concepts and abilities. There is some self-exploration, but your impression is that the courses move on to the notion of leadership relatively rapidly, with less emphasis on self-exploration as a leader. However, in the author's opinion, who you are is the most important component in defining the type of leader you will be. Your training as integrated coaches supports this viewpoint. You strive to figure out who you are and what it entails for your leadership style and decisions. When you engage with your executive customers to help them develop their businesses.

A leader should ask, "What opposing values and power conflicts exist in this scenario, and how will I consider the complete context in assisting others in navigating the difficulty at hand?"

Now is the moment for businesses to build leaders who can adjust themselves and their organizations to deal with disruptions while doing their daily tasks. The ability of businesses to adjust to changing circumstances is critical. Disruptions can be viewed as a danger, which requires resistance, or as an opportunity, which requires adaptation. Adaptive organizations, according to Deloitte, will succeed. To become an adaptable company, large-scale global enterprises must make a fundamental shift in operating and management philosophy that allows them to function with a start-up mindset and drive current people practices that enable enterprise agility through an empowered network of teams. Leaders must leave their comfort zones and take on adaptive problems with no obvious answers in order to prepare for the future. Hierarchies must play a supporting role in enabling a constantly evolving network of teams. These groups require adaptable leaders.Leaders who are flexible, the way people live, work, and conduct business will continue to be shaped and reshaped by long-term upheaval and change. Adaptive firms must look beyond incremental development and address current practices' flaws on a regular basis. Adaptive leaders need to climb up on the roof from time to time to observe what's coming over the horizon. When they detect the potential for disruption, they must move rapidly to plan responses in concert with other leaders.

Leaders must analyze their behaviors and how they effect their companies as part of adaptive leadership training. HR can ensure that leaders learn from the past, adapt to the present, and prepare for the future by effectively transforming and demonstrating adaptive capacity. CEOs are afraid that their leaders will be unprepared to deal with expected challenges. They also desire greater results from their leadership development efforts. That entails creating adaptive leadership skills and providing them at an organizational level for the chief learning officer and learning and development professionals. There are two barriers preventing businesses from responding to new circumstances. First, hierarchical arrangements, for starters, stifle team effectiveness by reducing decision-making and communication. Second, the majority of team leaders are actually process managers who are at ease in their technical operations zone but uncomfortable when there are disturbances. They attempt to apply operational abilities to adaptive obstacles, but instead of generating fresh solutions, they resort to patching problems.

Does your company's culture value and promote learning from mistakes?

Is it possible for CEOs to take frequent breaks from activity to find time for reflection and renewal? This is the questions that organizations that seek to promote executive flexibility should ask. Organizations will be able to build the leadership talent needed to effectively handle significant strategic problems if these questions are well addressed. Individual and organizational performance will soar to new heights as a result of adaptable leadership.

One of adaptive leadership's strengths is also one of its limitations. For the most part, an adaptable leader must place less value on structure in order to efficiently execute change. Some employees, on the other hand, thrive in regimented workplaces, and adaptive leadership would be a poor match for them. An adaptable leader will attempt to provide some structure for those employees that require it. Nonetheless, in this unstructured work environment, there are still possibilities for individuals to be less productive. It's in the nature of rules to be broken. An ethical leader may squirm after seeing how an adaptable leader operates. Ethical leaders support an organization's policies because they correspond with their own personal beliefs. An adaptable leader, on the other hand, may bend (or even break) the laws within the bounds of the law in order for the business to undertake the most effective change plan feasible.

Adaptive leaders are always looking for new methods to match pivotal events with shifting consumer preferences. They are attempting to alter client preferences in ways that benefit both their companies and their customers. They train their employees for both expected and unexpected outcomes. They can feel when things are about to change and react rapidly. These adaptable leaders are able to function effectively, adapt rapidly, invent new methods of working, and alter their businesses in a seamless manner. Organizations must produce leaders who can adjust themselves and their organizations to deal with challenges now.

Describe the technical and interpersonal skills you've developed as a result of your leadership development. Ensure that articulated purpose and talent management executives are enabled by competences. Explain the stages of leadership competency for different types of leaders, such as individual contributors, subject matter experts, project managers, executives, people leaders, high performers, and emerging executives. Incorporate expected outcome delivery into recruiting, onboarding, learning and development, and performance management methods. Ensure that thought leaders' leadership approaches are tailored to your organization's goals.

Adaptive leaders are always looking for new methods to match pivotal events with shifting consumer preferences. They are attempting to alter client preferences in ways that benefit both their companies and their customers. They train their employees for both expected and unexpected outcomes. They can feel when things are about to change and react rapidly. These adaptable leaders are able to function effectively, adapt rapidly, invent new methods of working, and alter their businesses in a seamless manner. Organizations must produce leaders who can adjust themselves and their organizations to deal with challenges now.

Leadership barriers to adaptive capacity changing one's conduct in reaction to adversity does not come easily for many business executives. While most business executives are competent and clever, it can be challenging to acquire new behavioral reactions when their previous habits match their businesses' goals in the majority of circumstances. Introducing new behavioral options is typically unsettling, and it may make leaders feel exposed. People tend to cling to practices that have served them well in the past, which might limit their ability to change. Rather than waiting for agility to spread from the bottom up, HR executives must support and assist leaders in taking command of their transitions. These techniques can aid in the development of an adaptable leadership style.

Many firms managed to modify their operations models throughout the pandemic, according to McKinsey & Co., with the development of remote work. Businesses that had a successful transformation were more likely to perform in the top quartile of their peers. Businesses that did not invest in change, on the other hand, fared the poorest. This just goes to demonstrate that adaptability is the key to future success. It's vital to remember that adaptive capability is a continuum. Some leaders (and organizations) are considered inherently nimble, while others must work hard to improve their adaptability. However, in the long term, the efforts to overcome any barriers will be worthwhile. All HR executives need to do now is get the rest of the firm on the same page.

First, HR executives must explain why agility and flexibility are so important for success, and leaders must recognize the need of adaptive capability leadership. Then, and only then, should executives be encouraged to think about the company's operational model. Is it assisting and connecting teams rather than hindering them? Is it going to pave the road for a prosperous future? Finally, HR professionals should collaborate with corporate leaders to guarantee that the transition takes fewer than 18 months to accomplish. This, according to McKinsey & Co., will maintain momentum and prevent the organization from becoming exhausted.One such disruption is the proliferation of consumer options and the use of digital technology to differentiate them. It brings with it new opportunities as well as new problems. It's not enough to use digital technology on the periphery.

"The improvisational ability to lead adaptively relies on responding to the present situation rather than importing the past into the present and laying it on the current

situation like an imperfect template. Knowing how the environment is pulling your strings and playing you is critical to making responsive rather than reactive moves."— Ronald Heifetz

Many of the modifications you made necessitated finding the correct balance of elements, maintaining tensions, and avoiding either or thinking. What Do Adaptive Leaders Do? They made continuous improvement approaches work by giving them a purpose, fostering the necessary dispositions in adults, and providing the time, political space, relational environment, and learning culture. Developing a shared goal like this necessitates a high level of leadership ability. Finding something that fits perceived needs, is compatible with the expectations of the external world, and advances the improvement agenda ahead is the skill of determining the focus of an endeavor. Sometimes the purpose emerges from the needs of team and it's leader; in this case, the leader's responsibility is to listen and distill some shared aims, much like a community organizer might. The motivation might come from anywhere.

Consider yourself the HR Director of a corporation with a significant turnover rate. Employees that are highly trained and competent are leaving the company for rivals, which has a negative impact on the bottom line. What strategy would you use to tackle this problem? If you approach this scenario as a technological problem, you might be inclined to use technical solutions to fix it. Perhaps you require a new incentive scheme to keep your top employees? Perhaps they require more frequent rewards? Perhaps their bosses aren't doing a good job of encouraging and engaging them, and they need to improve.

You could attempt these remedies and discover that they either don't work or just work for a short period of time.

The corporate culture has been engrained with a lack of accountability and a tendency to blame others for missed deadlines. The HR personnel, as well as the team managers, were part of the problem. To transform the culture, input from the whole organization was solicited. Clearly, there were difficulties and disagreements during the process, and suggested modifications were greeted with opposition from many in top-tier management and teams across many departments. Instead, businesses must figure out how teams naturally connect with one another and with customers, and then create multidisciplinary teams, communities, reporting relationships, and communication channels to enable such interactions.

If you want to overcome this challenge as an adaptable leader, you'll need to enlist the help of the whole organization in transforming the culture. As a result of this process, there will almost certainly be a lot of awkward conversations, disagreements, and roadblocks. You'll have to give the leadership team difficult feedback while also being open to receiving it yourself. It's possible that you'll have to cope with your own anxieties and disappointments. It will take time for the shift to take hold, and it will almost certainly be greeted with resistance from a variety of sources. However, you will only be able to effectively solve this difficulty if you go through this procedure.

The vision of the company should be aligned with and served through learning. If you are the CEO of your firm, you must consider yourself the chief learning officer and ask four questions. First, how do your systems enable organizational learning? Second, how can a person communicate with the organization what they've learnt?

Third, how can you use technology to help with learning and knowledge distribution within your organization? last, what procedures have you put in place to gather and respond to input from both internal and external stakeholders in your organization? Finally, feedback-based organizational learning enhances capability. In addition, capacity must be quantified. This means that you must eventually devise a metric for measuring the effectiveness of your capacity in terms of mission enablement. When you work with your executive clients to help them become more adaptable leaders, you start by figuring out who they are—what their personality type is, how they handle stress, how they communicate, what they value, and so on. All of this is in the service of gaining a better understanding of themselves as individuals and then implementing the notion of leadership in light of that knowledge.

For example, Jeff Bezos is well-known for his conviction that meetings centred on PowerPoint did not result in greater capability to carry out their purpose. As a result, he devised the Narrative Meeting Process. He redesigned meetings such that they were focused on a four-to-six-page evidence-based narrative memo that was written before each meeting. He then set aside the first 20 minutes of the meeting to read the material, followed by a substantial discussion and debate in which he questioned the presenting team rigorously. While this change may appear to be logistical or even trivial, it was not. It resulted in the instant sharing of the same. It resulted in an immediate sharing of the same mental model of the situation at hand, resulting in better informed judgments and organizational success. So, while considering capability, you must consider four factors. First, consider what capabilities and systems are required to assure the success of your mission.

Then, consider a team, process, or system in your business and consider how each of these contributes to mission capability. Third, identify how you'll acquire honest criticism that you can use to improve your skills. This is accomplished by linking an organization's capabilities to its learning systems. Finally, ask yourself how convinced you are that all of your organization's processes are creating the capability to carry out your purpose.

Power Points

- The ability of businesses to adjust to changing circumstances is critical.
- Leaders must leave their comfort zones and take on adaptive problems with no obvious answers in order to prepare for the future.
- You can't learn unless you fail, and you can't achieve until you face obstacles.
- You strive to figure out who you are and what it entails for your leadership style and decisions.

CHAPTER SIX

CHANGE CHAMPION

Adaptive Or Agile Leaders Champion The Team.

"The reasonable man adapts himself to the world; the unreasonable one persists in trying to adapt the world to himself. Therefore all progress depends on the unreasonable man." George Bernard Shaw

Change is unavoidable. An adaptable leader isn't surprised by change. Instead, this leader has put in place procedures and tactics to deal with problems as they emerge. When an adaptable leader is present, at least one backup plan is always easily available. You are living in an era of both peril and opportunity. To merely live, individuals, businesses, communities, and countries must constantly adapt to new circumstances. People in all sectors are being called upon to lead with the confidence and skill to question the status quo, deploy themselves with agility, and organize others to go into the unknown because they want more and want to prosper even in continuously shifting and often risky conditions. Adaptive leaders know how to invent alternate uses of things to promote their vision, just as core and effective leaders know how to identify what should and shouldn't work. Core leadership, equals book smarts, successful leadership equals street smarts, and adaptable leadership means inventiveness. To put it another way, core leaders are recognized for their competency, successful leaders for their expertise, and adaptable leaders for their visions with flexible paths. Be tenacious. The greater the level of uncertainty, the more untrainable leadership development is infused. Because of the speed at which change occurs, companies must learn more quickly, more thoroughly, and more extensively than ever before. Focusing solely on guiding the moment and directing the future is no longer sufficient. Rather, every activity, strategy, job, and communication should be part of a continuous cycle of improvement and iteration.

Because of the epidemic, the way you work has changed, and leaders must adapt accordingly. While some companies have chosen to remain with remote work, others have chosen a hybrid strategy that includes some in-office time. The shift in the work model has posed a challenge to hybrid leadership. As a result, leaders will need a new set of abilities to keep their employees engaged and productive in the new hybrid workplace. New management issues have arisen as a result of the hybrid work approach. Improved leadership abilities that can adapt to changing work conditions are required by the new hybrid model. Upskilling has become more important for better leadership. In a hybrid culture, leaders must continually develop, learn, and unlearn. Leaders should draw on prior experiences to develop the leadership abilities necessary in a hybrid work environment, even if it has been a learning process for everyone. This may be accomplished through leadership development programs that are specifically geared to promoting strong leadership that is necessary for enhancing workplace culture. Build trust in the workplace. In this climate, managers demand more adaptable leadership management, which can be done through a variety of leadership development programs that will assist the organization in going to the next level.

"Notwithstanding the challenging societal circumstances at this moment presented by the Omicron surge, CEOs remain optimistic about the business environment and see strong growth opportunities over the next year. A new normal appears to be setting in whereby business leaders simply expect new challenges to arise continuously, and are confident they can manage through them to achieve positive business results while making a real difference in society." — Joe Ucuzoglu, Chief Executive Officer, Deloitte US

Leadership is the responsibility of everyone, and it is assumed by the individual who is best positioned to make a decision or take action. Allowing leadership to be distributed is at the heart of adaptive leadership. Adaptive leaders develop employees who can foresee what will happen, prepare for it, adjust to it, recover from setbacks, and keep going even when things are difficult. The adaptive leader must demonstrate resilience on a daily basis so that the capacity to handle adversity, remain cheerful and hopeful, and respond calmly to difficult events pervades the business. Adaptive leaders instill a feeling of common purpose in their teams and govern by influence rather than by command and control. Leadership must be adaptable in the face of volatile, uncertain, complex, and ambiguous change. Adaptive leaders must be able to determine when to enter the conflict and when to exit and observe from the sidelines.

As a leader, you must help people realize how what they gain is crucial to their basic beliefs and how the change will aid in the evolution of their traditions rather than depreciate them. Adaptive leaders have a deep awareness of each employee's strengths and weaknesses, and they manage them appropriately. Adaptive leaders have a high level of flexibility, i.e., the capacity to seamlessly go from traditional to adaptive leadership styles. Adaptive leaders are driven to achieve excellent results and to infuse their enthusiasm and fire into their teams. Because they expect plans to alter, adaptive leaders always have contingency plans in place. Adaptive leaders use quick, fluid communication to keep everyone on the same page. They also encourage team participation, which inevitably leads to fewer mistakes and higher quality work. They build trust and provides psychological stability for the people it leads, allowing them to continue to learn, grow, and contribute to a shared future. Adaptive leadership recognizes that the whole is more than the sum of its parts in the proper Aristotelian sense. That the organization as a whole will perform better when each employee feels safe, confident, and trusted by their leadership. Adaptive leadership, when done well, instills togetherness, ambition, and resilience in a team.

Adaptive leadership is to find a middle ground where the business, external stakeholders, and rivals can all benefit from the solutions you provide. This may seem counterintuitive if you're used to working simply as a competitor, but if you and your competitors can support each other, it'll be well worth your time and money. Another fundamental element of adaptive leadership is to promote and nurture an honest culture. Adaptive executives are well-versed in the finest policies that can be implemented to help the company. They can also efficiently execute such rules in a way that people accept them. Every employee feels appreciated and respected because their thoughts and ideas are heard and considered. As more new ideas are presented, this has a ripple effect across the business. This encourages more buy-in, which is necessary for the solution's effective implementation. Adaptive leadership should provide their staff with the most up-to-date technologies to increase efficiency and production while reducing time and effort spent on various activities.

They will view losing a game as a learning experience, and the squad will regroup and prepare for the next game. They will be able to empathize with others and put themselves in their position to comprehend their point of view. Players are encouraged to take responsibility and make decisions. Adaptive leaders are open to change and embrace it. It's the truth for them. They form dynamic teams that welcome change and use cooperation and communication to transform any uncertainty into great outcomes. Adaptive leaders state their intentions openly and then let the participants play the game. The participants will either win or lose the game in the end. Adaptive leadership isn't about having a lot of power. It's about developing a feeling of organizational accountability in the whole workforce. Learning is impossible without some risk and failure. While conventional leaders may seek for green lights on the dashboard progress report, adaptive leaders encourage individuals to be open about where they've pushed themselves and where they may be struggling—the truth. Adaptive leaders encourage teams to generate outcomes by empowering people, and they give lots of praise and celebration for the team's achievement.

They share the limelight with the squad and ensure that they get lots of favorable press for their work.

In order to make positive changes happen, senior leaders must first be open to suggestions from employees at all levels. Mid-level supervisors must coach employees on how to convey ideas and information in a compelling manner. Everyone must believe they are capable of bringing about change. Everyone must feel comfortable discussing or disagreeing about what is going on. At every stage of the game, employees must know how to be informal leaders. Naturally, in a dysfunctional workplace, an intimidating individual or someone who dominates the discourse might obstruct this. The adaptive leader is once again called upon to teach and assist all employees in developing the skills necessary to deal with dysfunctionality in an emotionally intelligent and caring manner. By doing so, he or she is equipping workers with the communication tools they need to get beyond these disruptive situations, as well as ensuring that all viewpoints are valuable to the company and that all voices count, even those who aren't conscious of their impact.

Workplaces and settings are always changing. Because your workload, team members, clients, and resources are always changing, your leadership and management style must change as well. Allowing your team to have fun at work is one way to guarantee that they adjust to the shift and continually offer the ideas that matter. Allow them to laugh out loud during cooperation calls to lighten the tone. Alternatively, pick an alternative venue for brainstorming, such as an office park or a company lunch. Also, be open to all ideas rather than dismissing them as *"dumb."* Remember that a funny or *"dumb"* concept that makes it to a brainstorming session might transform into a fantastic out-of-the-box idea with more discussion. Even when faced with uncertainty, leaders who challenge current conventions, ask questions, and arrange dispute resolution assist the company in overcoming any challenge and emerging victorious.

Many changes entail adaptation issues that require people to develop new skills. In corporate and community transformation attempts, this is frequently disregarded. People must adapt to address challenges in order for the shift to be effective. Adapt or change is required of both leaders and individuals. Individuals must develop their own capacity to solve issues and capitalize on opportunities. Many of your greater societal crises, such as climate change, do not have a technology solution to transition from individual to systemic challenges. You need people to modify what they do until there is a technological answer, and you need to address the bigger adaptive issues involved in making these adjustments, which include, among other things, value systems and identity. Leaders must mobilize their followers to modify existing habits and build new ones. Adaptive leaders keep their heritage alive by refining or evolving it. If this growth hurts relationships , the ties must be renegotiated as part of the transformation process. Deeply held beliefs and identities may be impacted by these shifts. If these values and identities are thoroughly and compassionately addressed, change may strengthen rather than weaken the foundation on which the company or community was created.In the transition process, each team member plays an important role.

Adaptive leaders have productive and friendly relationships with their coworkers. Adaptive leaders and their teams routinely look outside the box rather than sticking to tried-and-true techniques. Adaptive leadership necessitates a high level of self-awareness on the part of the leaders, as well as an understanding of how their verbal and non-verbal communication affects the team. Making errors is a natural part of the process. Nobody can accomplish everything perfectly the first time. Accepting mistakes, learning from them, and making course changes are all part of adaptive learning. Teams and organizations must evaluate their performance on a regular basis, identifying strong and weak areas and making modifications to improve results. Continuous learning and progress are the names of the game on other planets.

A successful, adaptable leader recognizes this and places team members in locations that allow their individual abilities to flourish. They also give resources to help build and maintain these strengths. An adaptable leader does not reward a team member for their pleasant working relationship. This leader, on the other hand, awards prizes depending on performance. In the transition process, each team member plays an important role. A successful, adaptable leader recognizes this and places team members in locations that allow their individual abilities to flourish. They also give resources to help build and maintain these strengths. It's not about keeping track of the number of hours or work performed in a day; it's about whether this team member can meet the deadline. Adaptive leadership has certain pacesetting streaks as a result of this. Furthermore, the incentives are not necessarily monetary. They range from providing employees with paid time off to year-long fellowships that help them advance professionally. In essence, rewards are also handled in an adaptive manner.

Leadership is a shared responsibility. Leadership cannot always be the responsibility of one person in a world of constant and volatile change. Of course, teams must be capable in order to be effective in solving their own problems. Employees benefit from both formal and embedded learning opportunities, such as work shadowing and job rotation, provided by great agile leaders. Adaptive leaders don't wait for a slowdown to grow their people—they know those are rare—instead, they use busy moments to stretch and challenge team members to contribute in new ways and through new responsibilities that stretch and challenge them. Adaptive leaders also make fair judgments, share knowledge, retain integrity, develop others, and continue to grow throughout their lives. Adaptive challenges are problems that experts are unable to solve. They necessitate in-house tests, findings, and changes. People must accept new values and attitudes, as well as absorb the change, in order to make the adaptive jump. Adaptive leaders lead with empathy, learn from their mistakes, accept change, and create conditions that benefit the greatest number of people. Adaptive leadership may help authority figures see the broad picture and delegate important work back to individuals and teams during times of crisis.

Nowadays, teams are formed swiftly and then disbanded just as quickly. They must promptly establish contact with the project leader, be given full authority to make choices, and complete the assignment. If agility is not fostered, inflexible leaders can severely slow down growth. The art of adaptive leadership is establishing the ideal environment for self-organization. An atmosphere in which agile teams cooperate, learn from one another, receive immediate feedback from users, and are committed to quality and continual improvement. He or she neither micromanages nor creates unlimited freedom for the individuals. In today's complicated VUCA settings, striking a balance between chaos and rigorous structure is critical. It might be difficult to create and maintain the ideal environment. Culture, ownership, mentality, feedback, and long-term objectives are all important. The leader must be able to handle a variety of situations, particularly new, changing, and ambiguous ones.

"We cannot address the problems with the same mindset that created them," Einstein observed.

You are to blame for our current circumstances. Here's something to think about for a bit. Your systems have been tuned to provide the results you're seeing now. If your work efforts are constantly over budget or late, you've established a system that not only produces these results, but it is optimized to produce them. You must modify the system in order to change the outcomes. An adaptable leader places a premium on value and respect. Each team member's input is valuable and appreciated. Adaptive leaders also take the time to listen. Adaptive leaders often think about the best way to bring change to their team rather than imposing it all on them all at once. There are several parallels to the affiliate leadership style. It is possible to make too many changes in a short period of time.

Leaders frequently state that they favor transparency. What they truly mean is that they want to know what their teams are up to all of the time. Leaders who are honest about their own work—sharing information about what they're working on, bigger corporate goals, and the priorities that should direct their teams' work—are required for agile leadership. Adaptive or Agile leaders make sure their staff are knowledgeable about the company's strategy and the context in which they operate, and then they step aside. Rather than checking in on their teammates, they check in. They also provide employees the freedom to work through concerns and solve problems.

For teams, agile leadership necessitates new levels of empowerment, enablement, and development. Agile teams are learning new work practices at the same time as executives who are ensuring success in the new agile environment. Feedback is an important aspect of adaptive development. Great adaptive leaders provide feedback while also empowering their teams to provide and accept input. They assist the team in maintaining contact with the organization in order to obtain critical feedback from internal customers and the firm as a whole. Agile leaders serve as mentors and coaches for the teams they manage. Customers must be involved in the process for agile work approaches to be successful. Great adaptive leaders make it easier for customers to participate. Consumers' expectations are defined, opportunities and workplaces where customers may be present are provided, and customers are given the time they require. In fact, adaptive leaders would not allow a team to start a project unless the customer was prepared to spend time with the team.

Measurement, monitoring, and management are all intertwined. Great adaptive leaders encourage teams to measure their own results in addition to tracking their own measures. They track factors like meeting time, number of projects, customer happiness, team trust, and more, in addition to velocity, the gold standard of agile measurement. They know how the team is doing so they can provide feedback, eliminate roadblocks, and create possibilities for growth. Working on one project at a time, for example, is an important aspect of agile. Leaders must sometimes push back on the business to ensure that agile teams are not overburdened and can thrive by prioritizing projects and outcomes. Performance is measured by adaptive leaders. Because agile is a new method of working in most organizations, outstanding adaptive leaders must educate the rest of the organization on work procedures, eliminate barriers, and establish team boundaries. Working as a team, for example, is an important aspect of agile.

Adaptive leadership, as suggested by the author, poses a number of difficulties. Experimenting, learning new information, and making multiple modifications throughout your firm are all part of this leadership paradigm. You will only be able to maintain the changes and prosper if you modify your mindset and adjust your policies. Changing people's attitudes, beliefs, and perceptions, on the other hand, is frequently more difficult than flossing a cat's teeth. Making adjustments necessitates a degree of disloyalty to your past. If you wish to adopt a new marketing plan, for example, you must first accept the truth that your current marketing techniques are ineffective.

Another issue with adaptive leadership is that it creates an environment conducive to various types of opposition. This might be from your employees or other stakeholders in the organization. Stakeholder Any individual, group, or entity with an interest in an organization and the effects of its activities is referred to as a stakeholder in business. Marginalizing, distracting, and assaulting are the most prevalent techniques used to stymie adaptive change. If you see any of these behaviors, it's likely that your staff are resisting the new policy you're attempting to impose.

Adaptive leadership, poses a number of difficulties. Experimenting, learning new information, and making multiple modifications throughout your firm are all part of this leadership paradigm. You will only be able to maintain the changes and prosper if you modify your mindset and adjust your policies. While maintaining a positive environment, adaptive leadership may provide businesses with inventive and meaningful answers to challenging situations. Adaptive leadership necessitates the participation of all members of the organization. This implies adaptable leaders must urge everyone engaged to change their mentality and display adaptive leadership skills. Employees who prefer the status quo and have no desire to change the company may find this difficult.

The refusal of leaders to listen to other people's perspectives is perhaps the biggest obstacle posed by adaptive leadership. Adaptive leadership, as previously said, is more about cooperation than it is about power. Adaptive leaders, in principle, should be open to listening to and modifying suggestions made by coworkers or clients. In actuality, only a small number of leaders are prepared to listen to others who disagree with them. What such leaders fail to realize is that listening does not always imply forsaking one's own objectives. It simply implies that you have a better understanding of your employees' requirements. As a result, you'll be able to work more efficiently to implement modifications. Adaptive leaders foster a progressive and open-minded work environment. Errors are recognized as a necessary part of the process. Adaptive leaders recognize and embrace adversity. They get their team members ready to solve problems. Adaptive leaders recognize that finding a long-term solution may take a few tries.

Hesitancy change can only be successful if everyone in the organization is involved in its execution. Some employees may be unwilling to execute a new approach because it requires them to master a new method or alters the nature of their work. It is possible that a new strategy will be unsuccessful if it is not applied across the whole organization. Adaptive leadership transfers authority and influence from a few top-level executives to all employees. Some top-level workers who are accustomed to wielding a great deal of decision-making authority may find it difficult to give control to the entire group. Adaptive leaders value relationships as much as they value money.This knowledge aids them in ensuring that organizational members and other stakeholders are on board with any long-term changes. Although adaptive leadership demands a significant amount of work, it pays off handsomely. Adaptive businesses, according to trustworthy statistics, reap enormous financial and operational benefits. Even during moments of turbulence, they are able to withstand storms and surge to the top.

Adaptive leadership depends on the ability to bring together a broad collection of individuals to explore ideas and develop practical solutions. Long-term results are improved when there are more ideas. Team members can also benefit from one another's knowledge and experience by gaining some personal and professional growth. Adaptive leaders adopt a democratic leadership style rather than a hierarchical one in this way. For the adaptable leader, rules serve as a guideline rather than a strict manner of doing things. This leader is intent on attaining the best possible result in the most efficient manner possible. It may even become clear that the present regulations aren't working for the company and need to be changed.

An adaptable leader places a premium on value and respect. Each team member's input is valuable and appreciated. Adaptive leaders also take the time to listen.

Adaptive leaders often think about the best way to bring change to their team rather than imposing it all on them all at once. There are several parallels to the affiliate leadership style. It is possible to make too many changes in a short period of time. An adaptable leader may terminate a failing initiative before it has a chance to prosper. This may not sit well with certain team members, resulting in a schism among the organization's members. Discord is an impediment to successful transformation. Adaptive leaders stay on top of the current trends so that they have a variety of methods to choose from when change is required. All strategies will fail to achieve the goals set by the leader. The leader, on the other hand, can swiftly adjust and identify the best approach for the situation.

The adaptable leader recognizes that change is a difficult process. As a result, he or she can anticipate and counteract any hesitant conduct on the part of colleagues. A recognition that large-scale change is a slow process that needs patience and a willingness to withstand the pressure that comes with it. Adaptive leaders understand that change takes time and are willing to put in the time required to build a better organization. Adaptive leaders are proactive in their approach. They detect problems and spend whatever resources are required to remedy them ahead of time. Adaptive leaders are at ease with the unknown.They understand that not having a quick solution to an issue is an important element of the positive transformation process. Adaptive leaders enjoy experimenting with new ideas and solving problems. They are ready to evaluate their work and make adjustments as needed. They recognize that handling nebulous and difficult topics necessitates trial and error. Adaptive leaders connect long-term corporate objectives to systematic transformation. Action is conducted with the goal of achieving a certain outcome in mind.

Adaptive leadership, like all leaders, is concerned with making big decisions. But what sets them apart as leaders is that they are open to input, prepared for inevitable change, adept at adapting to new situations, and flexible enough to reverse course when necessary. In terms of difficulty, adaptive leadership can be distinguished. A technological problem may have a one-time solution, but an adaptive problem requires time and may necessitate organizational culture changes. The latter occurs when a firm is in transition (for better or worse, such as expansion or downsizing) and needs to adjust its long-term business plans. Leadership that emphasizes being ready and eager to work on changes has a lot of success.

If you want to be an adaptable leader, you need to study, apply, and display four qualities: character, organizational justice, growth, and emotional intelligence. You have an excellent knowledge of your feelings and the feelings of people around you if you have high emotional intelligence. You can respond to your team in a fair, calm, and compassionate manner if you have acquired emotional intelligence. Of course, there are many aspects to emotional intelligence, and being sympathetic, searching for emotional reactions, respecting people's feelings, and adjusting your actions to their feelings can bring you a long way in this area. Despite the fact that an adaptable leader isn't scared to disobey the rules, he or she has a strong personality. This leader takes delight in being open, honest, and resourceful. The team respects the leader for owning up to his or her faults and making the appropriate decisions to repair them. The blame game isn't something an adaptable leader has time for.

"All fixed set patterns are incapable of adaptability or pliability. The truth is outside of all fixed patterns." -Bruce Lee

Several times in your career, you've been required to lead in an uncertain atmosphere. Situations in which everyone looked to you to make single-point-of-failure judgments based solely on your presumptions. During times of increased danger, the doctrine and chain of command were developed to support you via empirical direction. Many of the circumstances in which you were entrusted to serve proved to be much more challenging for your predecessors, who were well-known as excellent leaders. Unfortunately, the broad or core leadership style that your predecessors were known for failed miserably. Your success, was due to the growth of adaptable leadership. When things go bad, an adaptable leader helps stakeholders face the situation head-on rather than withholding. They encourage people to take part in problem-solving activities. People who are led by adaptable leaders are encouraged to think for themselves and make their own judgments. They also exhibit confidence in people's ability to solve difficulties successfully. Providing the right amount of direction and structure helps stakeholders feel confident in their decisions as they negotiate adaptive issues. An adaptive leader recognizes that ceding authority in this way allows out-group members to be more active, autonomous, and accountable for their own activities in the adaptive work of the organization and can create more commitment on their part. Adaptive leadership depends on the ability to bring together a broad collection of individuals to explore ideas and develop practical solutions. Long-term results are improved when there are more ideas. Team members can also benefit from one another's knowledge and experience by gaining some personal and professional growth. Adaptive leaders adopt a democratic leadership style rather than a hierarchical one in this way.

Power Points

- Adaptive leaders instill a feeling of common purpose in their teams and govern by influence rather than by command and control.
- Adaptive leadership isn't about having a lot of power.
- Adaptive leaders instill a feeling of common purpose in their teams and govern by influence rather than by command and control.
- Learning is impossible without some risk and failure.
- The refusal of leaders to listen to others is perhaps the most significant issue posed by adaptive leadership.
- An adaptable leader places a premium on value and respect.
- Adaptive leaders are open to a variety of viewpoints.

Final Thoughts

Organizations Must Exhibit An Adaptive Edge On A Regular Basis.

"Adaptability is not imitation. It means the power of resistance and assimilation."- Mahatma Gandhi

- Leaders must pay immediate attention to the aftermath of the pandemic problem, not just for present employees but also for new generations joining the workforce. Younger people are increasingly pressuring their employers to change their business models from linear to circular. If leaders do not respond in a comprehensive and constructive manner, they risk losing a whole generation of engaged brains who will gladly contemplate taking their skills elsewhere.

- Adaptive Leadership looks at business challenges through a fresh perspective, challenging standard leadership approaches that have reigned in businesses for years. Adaptive leaders can create dynamic teams that embrace change and convert uncertainty into opportunities. While some people are born with the ability to alter leadership styles, others must learn and practice the behaviors of great adaptable leaders.

- Communication is one of the most significant problems of the hybrid work paradigm, and it has resulted in a trust gap between employees and supervisors. While trust is important in all relationships, it is especially important in the workplace. As a result of the new hybrid working style, employees are reevaluating their relationships with their employers. If leadership does not respond to this new reality, there is a significant danger of trust breakdown and attrition.

- Adaptive leadership is all about supporting, experimenting with, and implementing change, whether it comes in the form of policy or attitudes. Many individuals may feel frightened when you push through substantial changes that force you to confront people's accustomed worlds. However, as a leader, you must figure out a way to make it work.

- No one is an island, and organizations and the individuals who work in them are no different. Authenticity improves a leader's relatability, humility, and ability to evolve in step with the demands of their business. Adaptive leaders display vulnerability and compassion instead of actively boosting their perceived authority in times of uncertainty, providing psychological safety for their team members to do the same. When people feel secure being themselves and taking risks, their performance rises. Because all three are basic psychological needs, their performance is likely to increase even more if colleagues' needs to feel competent, linked, and autonomous are acknowledged, understood, and met.

- It's never been more crucial to provide people and teams with the tools they need to succeed—to reach their full potential and optimize their skills. Organizations may increase their paths to success by identifying leadership as a characteristic existing in everyone of us rather than a duty for one individual to fulfill. One individual cannot possibly possess the depth and breadth of talent, knowledge, or insight required to navigate our rapidly changing future—and there is no expectation that they will under adaptive leadership. Adaptive leadership uses its collective spirit to create internal and external networks, collaborations, and interactions.

- Finding and pursuing a greater purpose becomes even more important in uncertain times. A common purpose, backed by a set of shared values, may assist companies enhance focus, cohesiveness, and resilience. When team members are connected, working toward the same goal, and confident in their organization's cohesive thinking, they are more likely to tackle complicated challenges together. A clear shared purpose and values may comfort employees about an organization's overarching objective, instill a feeling of ownership across its teams, and, as a result, inspire better performance.

- Leadership in the future will not be *"one size fits all."* Organizations must be prepared to adapt, bend, learn, and listen as the rate of change continues to accelerate. Leaders must understand the requirements of their employees, customers, markets, and the environment in order to lead in ways that meet, surpass, and harmonize with ever-changing expectations.

- You seek to provide businesses and leaders with clarity on adaptive leadership as well as the skills to fully embrace future change. You assist them in incorporating environmental, social, and governance factors into their operational models. You could rely on the stable assumption that the present and future will in some ways mimic the past in periods of slower change. This type of linear thinking lacks the breadth and depth required to navigate the future, let alone guide others through it.

- If the appropriate conditions for personal learning are in place, leaders can enhance their adaptability. A powerful learning process is created when challenging assignments are joined with opportunities to reflect with people who are willing and able to provide honest and constructive feedback, coaching, and support.

- Individuals and organizations can discover how to strengthen the critical executive capability of adaptability through a continuous learning culture. Opportunities for assessment, practice of new behaviors in conjunction with ongoing support and encouragement, timely feedback, and rewards for the development and execution of innovation and business performance improvement are all part of successful leadership and organizational development strategies.

- Adaptive leadership is greeted with a lot of opposition and requires a lot of effort, but the outcomes are well worth it. Organizations that adopt adaptive leadership reap considerable financial and operational benefits. When everyone's talents and abilities are utilized as part of a team effort, it leads to more pleasant working conditions, greater intra-team bonds, and healthier client connections.

- Individuals who rely on a short-term fix to meet a specific demand may be able to survive for the time being. However, in order to achieve long-term success and development, organizations must continue to change—quickly and at scale—in order to fulfill larger market and consumer expectations. Businesses that are really adaptable are those that understand their consumers, conduct trials, and focus on achieving outsized results. Finally, despite excellent intentions, businesses confront a variety of problems in implementing their plans and meeting their goals, including a lack of customer awareness owing to disconnected data and increased consumer expectations for better digital experiences.

- Leading organizations must exhibit an adaptable edge and update their business strategy on a regular basis. How do critical organizations create adaptive advantage at the most fundamental level? Building technology-base adaptive advantage successful species in biological ecosystems that are subject to extremely dynamic conditions are those that can adapt. Rapid adaptation necessitates creatures seeing more, thinking quicker, and reacting socially in their environment. Increasing the competitiveness of technology transformation companies are investing in technological efforts in order to develop new business models and increase efficiency. Without a doubt, technology has aided in the formation of some of the world's most profitable corporations.

- In this traditional system, the highest layer of management is normally responsible for identifying the proper answers. The top layer of management is frequently viewed as a single entity that will give order, direction, and protection. Order, direction, and protection are all crucial characteristics of leadership, but they do not define it. Someone who can lead people through adaptive changes is referred to as a leader. Leadership is not guided by a single person, but by a group of people working together to achieve a common purpose. When confronted with a problem for which there is no one-size-fits-all solution, adaptive leadership becomes critical.

- Keeping an eye on your rival is unavoidable. You must actively research how well they are responding to change, as well as how far behind or ahead of them you are. Business leaders must prioritize and encourage flexibility as a must-have organizational quality if they want to position themselves for long-term success in an ever-changing market. Traditional metrics of corporate health are no longer sufficient. To become adaptive now and survive tomorrow, the focus must be on shifting viewpoints and morphing swiftly and at scale.

About The Author

Dr. Amit is the founder of Accumentor India, a consultancy firm set up by him in the human resource solution space, which is focused on developing processes for people. It offers consultancy in learning management, mentorship, performance coaching, training and development, psychometric analysis, HR processes and interventions. He was formerly the Director of Expertell Learning Point.

Dr. Amit Das is an experienced sales, training, and learning professional with more than 20 years of working history in the healthcare, medical devices, and learning management industries. Dr. Amit is a seasoned training professional with rich experience and a successful track record in aligning learning and training solutions to key business strategy with a strong focus on flawless execution excellence to facilitate individual, business divisional, and organisational performance. He keeps relentless focus on measuring training impact and ROI, people capability building graphs, training process governance, performance coaching, and strategic thinking. These have been some of his key individual success traits. His core capabilities include performance coaching, designing training and development frameworks and facilitation of technical skill building, psychometric assessment and analysis, competency framework development and assessments, content design and facilitation of soft skills and leadership programmes, E-Learning Platform development, Learning Management Systems, Learning Impact Measurement, Talent Analysis and Performance Management System Review, Performance Coaching and Counselling.

His interests are in the areas of leadership development, coaching competency, mentorship, and motivational complexities related to organisational issues. His hobbies include public speaking, content creation, and reading books.

He has a Ph.D. and a Fellowship in strategic learning, along with his first class degrees in Human Resource Management and Corporate Laws from the top business schools in India. He is a certified professional coach from U.K. and behavioral coach from U.S.A.

References

- *Leadership: Theory and practice. Los Angeles, CA: SAGE Publications, Inc by Northouse, P. published 2019*
- *All Systems Go: The Change Imperative for Whole System Reform (Paperback)by Michael Fullan, published 2010*
- *The Constructivist Leader (Paperback) by Deborah Walker,published 1995*
- *Credibility: How Leaders Gain and Lose It, Why People Demand It (Paperback) by James M. Kouzes, published 1993*
- *Appreciative Leadership: Focus on What Works to Drive Winning Performance and Build a Thriving Organization (Hardcover) by Diana Whitney, published 2010*
- *Thinking, Fast and Slow (Hardcover) by Daniel Kahneman, published 2011*
- *The Checklist Manifesto: How to Get Things Right (Hardcover) by Atul Gawande, published 2009*
- *The Heart of Change: Real-Life Stories of How People Change Their Organizations (Hardcover) by John P. Kotter (Goodreads Author), published 2002*
- *Harvard Business Review on Leading Through Change (Paperback) by Harvard Business School Press (Compilation), published 2006*
- *Boards That Lead: When to Take Charge, When to Partner, and When to Stay Out of the Way (Hardcover) by Ram Charan, published 2013*
- *Innovation in the Schoolhouse: Entrepreneurial Leadership in Education (ebook)by Jack Leonard, published 2013*
- *Chaos, Complexity and Leadership 2012 (Hardcover) by Santo Banerjee (Editor), published 2013*

- *Checklist for Change: Making American Higher Education a Sustainable Enterprise (Hardcover)by Robert Zemsky, published 2013*
- *Nudge: Improving Decisions About Health, Wealth, and Happiness (Paperback) by Richard H. Thaler, published 2008*
- *Leverage Leadership: A Practical Guide to Building Exceptional Schools (Paperback) by Doug Lemov, published 2012*
- *Rethinking Leadership: A Collection of Articles (Paperback) by Thomas J. Sergiovanni (Editor), published 1999*
- *Leadership on the Line, With a New Preface: Staying Alive Through the Dangers of Change (Kindle Edition) by Ronald A. Heifetz*
- *We Want to Do More Than Survive: Abolitionist Teaching and the Pursuit of Educational Freedom (Hardcover) by Bettina L. Love, published 2019*
- *Solving Tough Problems: An Open Way of Talking, Listening, and Creating New Realities (Hardcover) by Adam Kahane (Goodreads Author), published 2004*
- *Change the World: How Ordinary People Can Accomplish Extraordinary Things (Hardcover) by Robert E. Quinn (Goodreads Author), published 2000*
- *Practical Approaches to Marketing Analytics in the Digital Age (ebook) by Cesar A. Brea, published 2012*
- *The Innovative University: Changing the DNA of Higher Education from the Inside Out (Hardcover)by Clayton M. Christensen, published 2011*
- *Reinventing Higher Education: The Promise of Innovation (Hardcover) by Ben Wildavsky (Editor), published 2011*
- *Bass & Stogdill's Handbook of Leadership: Theory, Research & Managerial Applications (Hardcover) by*

REFERENCES

Bernard M. Bass, published 1990

- *The practice of Adaptive Leadership: Tools and Tactics for Changing Your Organization and the world (Hardcover) by Ronald A. Heifetz, published 2009*
- *The Third Side: Why We Fight and How We Can Stop (Paperback) by William Ury, published 2000*
- *Accelerate: Building Strategic Agility for a Faster-Moving World (Hardcover) by John P. Kotter (Goodreads Author), published 2012*
- *How Colleges Change: Understanding, Leading, and Enacting Change (ebook) by Adrianna Kezar, published 2013*
- *Adaptation Studies and Learning: New Frontiers (Paperback) by Laurence Raw, published 2013*
- *More Than 50 Ways to Build Team Consensus (Paperback) by R. Bruce Williams, published 1993*
- *Adaptability: Responding Effectively to Change (Paperback) by Allan Calarco, published 2006*
- *Building Resiliency: How to Thrive in Times of Change (Paperback) by Mary Lynn Pulley, published 2001*
- *Playing to Win: How Strategy Really Works (Hardcover) by A.G. Lafley, published 2013*
- *Leadership Without Easy Answers (Hardcover) by Ronald A. Heifetz, published 1994*
- *Influencer: The Power to Change Anything (Hardcover) by Kerry Patterson, published 2007*
- *Leadership on the Line: Staying Alive Through the Dangers of Leading (Hardcover)by Ronald A. Heifetz , published 2002*
- *Leading for Powerful Learning: A Guide for Instructional Leaders (Paperback) by Angela Breidenstein, published 2012*
- *Theory U: Leading from the Future as it Emerges*

(Hardcover) by C. Otto Scharmer (Goodreads Author), published 2007

- *Complex Adaptive Leadership: Embracing Paradox and Uncertainty (Hardcover) by Nick Obolensky, published 2000*
- *Invaluable Master the 10 Skills You Need to Skyrocket Your Career by Maya Grossman, published 2020|*
- *Invaluable, Master the 10 Skills You Need to Skyrocket Your Career by Maya Grossman, published 2020*
- *The Effective Executive , The Definitive Guide to Getting the Right Things Done by Peter F. Drucker, Zachary First, Jim Collins, publish 2017*
- *The Leadership Challenge, How to Make Extraordinary Things Happen in Organizations by James M. Kouzes, Barry Z. Posner, published 2017*
- *Multipliers, How the Best Leaders Make Everyone Smarter by Liz Wiseman, Greg McKeown, published 2014*
- *The Leadership Gap, What Gets Between You and Your Greatness by Lolly Daskal, published 2017*
- *The Power of Positive Leadership, How and Why Positive Leaders Transform Teams and Organizations and Change the World by Jon Gordon, published 2017*
- *Wooden on Leadership, How to Create a Winning Organization by John Wooden, Steve Jamison, published 2005*
- *Learning Leadership, The Five Fundamentals of Becoming an Exemplary Leader by James M. Kouzes, Barry Z. Posner, published 2016*
- *5 Levels of Leadership, Proven Steps to Maximize Your Potential by John C. Maxwell, published 2013*
- *Real Leadership, 9 Simple Practices for Leading and Living with Purpose by John Addison, John David Mann, published|2016*

REFERENCES

- *TouchPoints, Creating Powerful Leadership Connections in the Smallest of Moments by Douglas Conant, Mette Norgaard, published 2011*
- *Organizational Culture and Leadership by Edgar H. Schein, published 2010*
- *The Practice of Adaptive Leadership, Tools and Tactics for Changing Your Organization and the World by Ronald A. Heifetz, Marty Linsky, Alexander Grashow, published 2009*
- *The Practice Of Adaptive Ledaership by Ronald A. Heifetz, Marty Linsky, Alexander Grashow*